A War of Nerves

A Veteran's Battle
With
PTSD and Injustice

Greg Hardin

To order additional copies of this book, contact:
Xlibris Corporation
1-888-795-4274
www.Xlibris.com
Orders@Xlibris.com
121533

PTSD

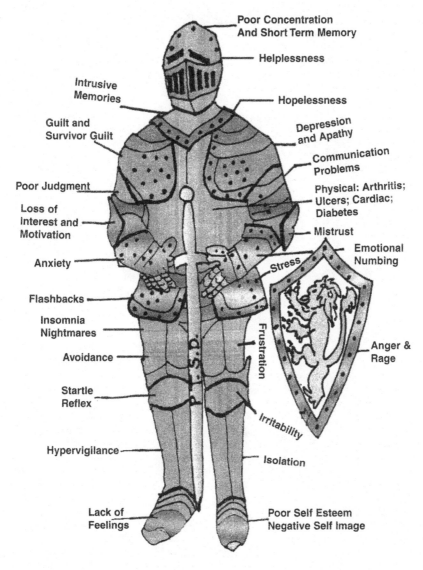

Poor Concentration And Short Term Memory

Helplessness

Intrusive Memories

Hopelessness

Guilt and Survivor Guilt

Depression and Apathy

Communication Problems

Poor Judgment

Physical: Arthritis; Ulcers; Cardiac; Diabetes

Loss of Interest and Motivation

Mistrust

Anxiety

Emotional Numbing

Stress

Flashbacks

Insomnia Nightmares

Frustration

Avoidance

Anger & Rage

Startle Reflex

Irritability

Hypervigilance

Isolation

Lack of Feelings

Poor Self Esteem Negative Self Image

R. GROVER 2002

Artist: Ralph Grover, RN, MSN

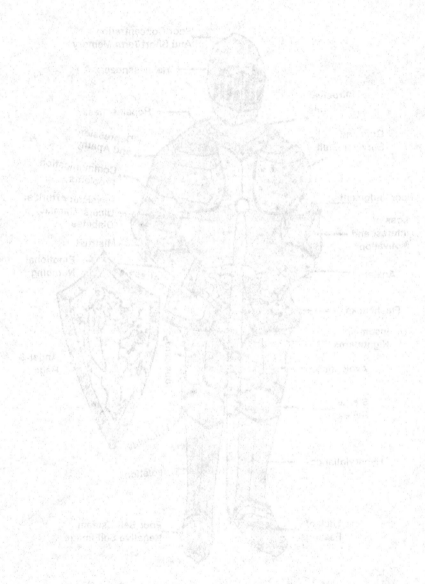

I dedicate this book to my father, a World War II veteran, and
to my grandfathers and four paternal uncles,
brave patriots who fought in World War II.
Special acknowledgment also goes to Brent
Tidwell, D.C. for his assistance and support.
And to the warriors of yesterday, today, and in perpetuity,
who valiantly sacrifice and defend our freedoms, I salute you.

Adjusting the doomsday clock

Since the doomsday clock was created in 1947, the hands have moved forward and back to reflect the state of international security.

1947
Seven minutes to midnight

The clock first appears on the cover of The Bulletin of the Atomic Scientists as a symbol of nuclear danger.

1968
Seven minutes to midnight

France and China acquire nuclear weapons. War rages in the Middle East, India and Vietnam. World military spending increases.

1981
Four minutes to midnight

The United States and the Soviet Union develop more nuclear weapons. Conflicts rage in Afghanistan, Poland, South Africa.

1949
Three minutes to midnight

The Soviet Union explodes its first atomic bomb.

1969
Ten minutes to midnight

The U.S. Senate ratifies the Nuclear Non-Proliferation Treaty.

1984
Three minutes to midnight

The arms race accelerates.

1953
Two minutes to midnight

The United States tested a hydrogen bomb in late 1952.

1972
Twelve minutes to midnight

The United States and Soviet Union sign the first Strategic Arms Limitation Treaty.

1988
Six minutes to midnight

The United States and the Soviet Union sign a treaty to eliminate intermediate-range nuclear forces.

1960
Seven minutes to midnight

International scientific cooperation and growing public understanding of the scope of nuclear weapons prompt the group to turn the clock back.

1974
Nine minutes to midnight

SALT talks break down. India develops a nuclear weapon.

1990
Ten minutes to midnight

The Cold War ends as democratic movements sweep eastern Europe. The clock has been redesigned to reflect the need for global security.

1963
Twelve minutes to midnight

The United States and Soviet Union sign the Partial Test Ban Treaty.

1980
Seven minutes to midnight

The SALT impasse continues. Terrorist actions are on the rise.

1991
Seventeen minutes to midnight

The United States and the Soviet Union sign the Strategic Arms Reduction Treaty and announce further weapons cuts.

Scientists set 'clock' forward

By TERRI LIKENS
The Associated Press

CHICAGO — Saying the threat of nuclear apocalypse did not disappear with the end of the Cold War, experts at the Bulletin of Atomic Scientists today pushed the hands of their famous "Doomsday Clock" three minutes closer to the hour of midnight.

"Unfortunately the world did not take full advantage of the opportunities available at the time," Leonard Rieser, chairman of the publication, said as he pushed the hands of the clock nearer to the hour that symbolizes nuclear apocalypse.

Rieser said the world remains "a very dangerous place."

The hands were reset to 14 minutes before midnight. They last were changed in 1991, at the end of the Cold War, to 17 minutes before midnight at the end of the Cold War.

Experts spent hours Thursday debating the threat and whether to change the time. It was the first time the Bulletin, marking its 50th year, debated the issue publicly, allowing questions and comment from the audience.

For some, nuclear science has already passed the threat stage.

"The clock's kind of ridiculous," Bob Rudner of the Alliance of Atomic Veterans told diplomats, physicists and others. "The face kind of gets in the way of the world. In terms of radiation victims, there are clocks ticking away inside of them."

Preface

Freedom is not free. Our wounded and disabled veterans know this more than anyone else. The price that we pay is indelible and searing – imprinted on our hearts and in the physical, psychological, and stress-related wounds that linger with us for a lifetime. I began my life as a patriot and I carry that legacy throughout time. Now, however, my physical and emotional pain outweighs the idealistic vision and definition of "service" that I entertained as a youth of eighteen. I survived, but the boy within me has died, his energy and enthusiasm subsumed in the reality of intense physical anguish and the effects of Nuclear-related Post Traumatic Stress Disorder ("PTSD"). A very motivated teen, intrigued by a family history of military involvement, that boy went the way of disillusionment, betrayed by a medical and legal system that turned away in his hour of need.

During the Cold War, I was there for my country when the Doomsday Clock (which connotes how close humanity is to catastrophic destruction, likely due to a nuclear holocaust) was four and three minutes until midnight – dangerously close to global disaster. Few civilians were aware just how close we were to a nuclear exchange with the Soviet Union. Having to serve in the role of nuclear deterrence (the credible threat of nuclear retaliation to forestall an enemy attack) altered my life in indescribable ways. As millions of lives hinged on a moment's notice, I tended to the machinery of the apocalypse.

The term "deterrence" is not a new concept. It was built into the United States Constitution, enshrined in the Second Amendment's right to bear arms, to maintain a balance of power. 24/7 vigilance is necessary to protect our freedoms, but how can we profess liberty and justice for all, when our men and women in service to our country are denied fair treatment under the law and are not provided with the proper medical care?

As a result of my sometimes overwhelming responsibilities as a Nuclear Systems Analyst, working with WMD's (weapons of mass destruction), I was transformed into someone I didn't recognize. At the outset, I was young and impressionable, right out of high school, carrying the emotional and physical weights of the entire globe. In the aftermath of that overwhelming experience, my stress-related injury, Nuclear-related PTSD, beset my every waking and sleeping moment. Transcending the boundaries of human capacity left me susceptible to involuntary modes of behavior – physical and emotional in nature – which caused me to relive the experience over and over again – as I do to this day. Consequently, in every respect, I became a shadow of myself.

Somehow, I had to rebuild my life, but each time I tried, my efforts were thwarted by the very institutions designed to protect every American citizen. Reinventing myself was virtually impossible – as it shall be for the rest of my life. Nuclear- and Combat-related PTSD - very real, documentable life-changing conditions - do not, simply, go away. I am constantly reminded of the permanence of my condition (Nuclear-related PTSD) in my everyday life, as I strive, in vain, to assimilate into a society that has, basically, betrayed me. In addition to all that I had to endure from my stress-induced symptoms, I had to deal with legal and medical care systems that constantly failed me. Therefore, my physical welfare, my professional livelihood, and my social relationships have been severely compromised.

I often think of our wounded veterans who have served their country, but are still deprived of good medical care and fair treatment under the law. By not providing such care and attention, our government and our society continue to perpetrate one of the worst crimes of our day.

John Donne, the 17th century English poet, said, "No man is an island entire of itself; every man is a piece of the continent, a part of the main...." For me, however, the "main" receded, leaving me to fend for myself, without recourse. I *am* an island.

Yet, I have a gift which fate and injustice never can never take from me: a voice with which to tell my story. In my microcosmic world, the truth of multitudes resonates. My hope is that my narrative will serve as an example to patriotic Americans, and inspire them to do their part in preserving liberty and justice for our wounded sons and daughters who defend our freedoms.

Chapter 1
Red, White and Blue Genetics

*T*he colors of the red, white, and blue flow through my veins; but my Post Traumatic Stress Disorder (PTSD) and physical torment are searing reminders of my deprivation of liberties. Such denials have entrapped me in a life not of my own choosing – a life of pain and dependence, devoid of freedom. Some have called me "a soldier of misfortune" but, as a Cold War veteran, my battle scars were not sustained on the front lines. Rather, the injuries that I received from working with weapons of mass destruction placed me on the frontier of personal warfare – one-on-one combat with my own body and the irrepressible forces of injustice, meted upon me by negligent, apathetic healthcare and legal systems.

I am a living testament to the harsh realities of PTSD, which result from exposure to a traumatic experience, and resurface in my everyday life. PTSD symptoms are as varied as the individuals who experience them. The disorder can manifest in the form of flashbacks, involuntary recollections of stressful events, and/or extreme emotional distress when faced with situations akin to the initial stressor. Conversely, the sufferer may experience a decrease in his or her level of responsiveness to stimuli, such as withdrawal, depression, a sense of hopelessness, or alienation from others. Other symptoms include, but are not limited to, hypervigilance, paranoia, exaggerated startle responses, and other physical effects in the aftermath of the initial trauma (e.g., perspiration, shortness of breath, or stomach ailments). Often, PTSD is correlated with experiences of physical pain and vice versa. However, in my case, my back pain and PTSD are unrelated. PTSD sufferers who have bodily pain or injury sometimes are desensitized, to the point of being able to withstand heightened levels of distress which would make functionality – and life itself – quite intolerable under so-called "ordinary" circumstances.

1

How I long to be "average" – to simply live every day without a heightened sense of my environment and everything around me – without paying heed to constant pain, which curtails my mobility and independence in ways that I never could have imagined in my young life! How I wish that I weren't called by circumstance and destiny to be Superman! I never set out to be superhuman. I simply aspired to follow in the footsteps of my father and four paternal uncles, consummate military men with unwavering faith in the ideals of freedom.

Varied and riveting, my uncles' experiences in service to our country shaped who I am. Their stories were recounted to me by my father and by my Uncle Seaborn (known to his family as "S.D."), whom I saw frequently in my youth and whose commitment to life in the military deeply impressed me. Beginning with Uncle Alton Hardin, the oldest of my father's brothers, the concept of service was genetically imprinted in my DNA. Alton was the first to pass away in 1967, when I was six years old. During World War II, he served in the army, and saw combat in Northern Africa and Sicily. After the war, he remained in the service for years, eventually rising to the rank of Captain. While in the army, he held a variety of jobs, which included his work in the Criminal Investigation Division ("the CID") and, later, in the Office of Special Investigations ("the OSI" which, for national security purposes, monitored me during and after my own service).

My father, Perry and his brother, Lowell Hardin (the latter of whom played softball in the South Pacific and, according to my father, was a good pitcher) also served, but never saw combat. Uncle S.D., however, served on the front lines and was most affected by World War II; hence, my enormous interest in him, especially. S.D. was part of the D-Day invasion at Normandy's Omaha Beach, and once was listed as missing in action. When my father later questioned his older brother's whereabouts during that time, S.D. simply replied, "Hell, I was digging a hole!" As I came to realize,

S.D. suffered from PTSD. He emerged from the war with signs of the disorder, which surfaced in such ordinary situations as riding a city bus. My father recalled one afternoon when the two rode the bus together in Washington D.C. (where my father had moved after graduating from high school in Tuscaloosa, Alabama). When the bus backfired, S.D. immediately went into response mode - as though the noise were the report of a rifle - and jumped down between the seats, flattening himself to the floor. Clearly, he was "shell-shocked" (the vernacular term of that era for PTSD). Uncle S.D. constantly spoke about and studied the war. I believe that his persistent preoccupation with his service was a catharsis, which enabled him to relive the past, put it behind him, and affirm his survival. Tragically, however, he ultimately succumbed to alcoholism and PTSD, never fulfilling his wish to revisit Omaha Beach with me. I still honor that proud expression of intent – and always will.

Uncle Brenton, who was three years older than my father, assumed the dangerous position of radio gunner on a low-flying B-24 Liberator bomber in the Naval Air Force during World War II. During the Korean War, he was called back into the service. Unlike S.D., he was not as vociferous or impassioned about his experiences. He also died, at age sixty-two, from liver failure, a consequence of alcoholism.

Right after graduating from high school in 1944, my father was destined for Washington D.C., where his older sister, Bertha, lived with her husband. Lured by the big city, the small-town Tuscaloosa boy had high hopes for his future. He took his first Civil Service job as a file clerk for the Secretary of Agriculture at that time, Claude Wickard. Toward the end of that year, the file room supervisor informed Dad of an opening for a file clerk job at the White House. Upon the supervisor's recommendation, he began in his new position at the beginning of 1945 – the year of President Roosevelt's final inauguration. Due to the president's failing health and the war, the swearing in ceremony was not publicized. However, because Dad had been detailed to the White House a few weeks earlier, he was invited to attend. Along with the rest of the White House staff, Dad looked on from the South Lawn, as Franklin D. Roosevelt and Harry S. Truman took their oaths of office, administered by Chief Justice Harlan F. Stone. President Roosevelt was so ill at the time, that he had to be body-lifted by Secret Service agents to be sworn in.

In that same year, 1945, before the Hiroshima and Nagasaki bombings, my father began working in the Truman White House as a file clerk handling the White House Central Files (now called "the General File"), consisting of policy-related and administrative matters. One year later, at age eighteen, he was drafted into the army and attained the rank of Corporal. The following year, in 1948, he returned to the White House, where he was promoted to working on the Official File and the President's Personal File (containing the president's personal correspondence and more sensitive documents). In 1950, Dad witnessed the events surrounding the assassination attempt on President Truman's life and the gruesome aftermath, in which one of the assassins and a White House police officer were killed.

Over the course of his remaining years in the File Office, Dad had first-hand access to many high-profile visitors to the White House. One such luminary was General Jonathan M. Wainwright, who valiantly assumed the Allied command in the Philippines from General Douglas MacArthur when the latter was reassigned to the Southwest Pacific. General Wainwright heroically resisted Japan's invasion of the Philippines, sustaining heavy losses and the surrender of seventy-thousand troops under General Edward King. By 1942, Wainwright and the Allied forces retreated to Bataan (a rocky extension of a mountainous region of the Philippines), where they were forced to surrender to the Japanese and make the Bataan Death March. In the aftermath of the surrender,

Wainwright remained in a Japanese prison camp until the end of the war, becoming that conflict's highest ranking POW. Wainwright's extraordinary bravery and selflessness earned him the Congressional Medal of Honor, bestowed by President Truman. Dad was present at the ceremony, and cherished the memory of meeting the eminent General.

By 1952, after resigning from his White House position, Dad decided to pursue his accounting degree, and took a job as a bookkeeper for a restaurant supply company. He then sought and obtained several credit union jobs in and around Washington D.C. before accepting a position at the Pentagon Credit Union. After his first marriage ended in 1954, he joined the Air Force, and worked in the payroll department. From 1955 to 1959, his traveled as a serviceman, primarily in Japan. When he returned to civilian life, he went back to Washington, D.C., where he worked at the Telephone Credit Union. There, he met my mother (his second wife) and, less than two years later, on October 17, 1961, I was born.

At the time, my family resided in Virginia, from where my father commuted to his job in D.C.. As he grew tired of the commute and yearned for a warmer climate, Dad eventually relocated us back home to Alabama when I was five. We lived close to the renowned BF Goodrich tire plant ("the Plant") in Tuscaloosa, where my father procured work as an accountant. Mom, Dad, my older half-brother, Donald and I had just welcomed my newborn sister, Nancy, into the family. All of us had to adjust to our new surroundings, particularly the pervading smell of rubber. As I reflect back on the smokestacks rising from the treetops, visible from our front yard, I realize that, at age five, I unwittingly beheld a harbinger of my future, when I, myself, would work at the Plant, and my life would change forever.

My childhood years were anything but carefree. Soon after our return to Alabama, my parents were drifting apart. My formative and teenage years were, therefore, spent somewhat itinerantly, as I traveled to northern California with Mom and my siblings to live with my maternal uncle. I was about seven or eight years old at the time. Before a year had passed, Dad came to drive me back home. Later, Mom took us to Kansas, where we resided with my maternal grandmother for about seven months. Restless and unhappy, I asked to return to Alabama. Mom called upon Dad, who came to take me home again. My father and I resided together, and my siblings later followed on their own. By Christmastime, 1978, I was back on familiar turf, taking odd jobs to save money, buying motorbikes and, generally, being a seventeen-year-old. Mom and Dad lived apart, and their marriage remained in an uncertain holding pattern.

As a teenager, I pivoted toward my father's side of the family, with whom I most identified. On holidays, my paternal family get-togethers were characterized by stories of public service and old photographs of my heroic uncles in their uniforms – the embodiments of sacrifice and valor. It was no wonder, therefore, that I decided to enter the service and perpetuate my red, white, and blue gene pool. My parents endorsed my decision, believing that it was appropriate and honorable. As for me, I realized that being in service to my country would provide me with the focus, stability and purpose that I craved. As my parents' marriage fell apart, shouldering the burdens of a directionless adolescence was very challenging for me. Because I wasn't encouraged to pursue an education beyond the twelfth grade, I went through the motions of learning without developing proper study habits. I simply wanted to find my niche in the world. My recruiter's offer of a job, therefore, came at just the right moment.

At the pinnacle of youth, vigor, and idealism, no one can have a true concept of war and its impact – let alone comprehend the awe-inspiring power of nuclear weapons. At eighteen, I thought that war occurred somewhere else – outside the purview of my life and everything that I knew. In my mind, there were two sides – a "winner" and a "loser" – with the reciprocal goal of conquering "the enemy." Never could I have conjured that this overly simplistic notion – along with my faith – would be challenged in immeasurable ways - and that I would, quite literally, hold the entire world in my hands.

Chapter 2
In the Dawn's Early Light

Spanning from 1945 to 1991, the Cold War was a very real phenomenon. The fact that it was not fought on the front lines, in hand-to-hand combat, does not mean that it played out in the esoteric realm of theory. On the contrary, the threat of nuclear annihilation faced by the two superpowers of that era – the United States and the Soviet Union – embroiled the world in perpetual fear of the apocalypse. The period was characterized by cycles of relative calm, juxtaposed by the threat of nuclear destruction. No one knew, at any given moment, when the force of either side would come to bear on the other. No matter what time the clock struck –in the dawn's early light or at midday, there was an endless uneasiness in the air that, to this day, has not escaped me.

At eighteen, the notion of an end-of-time scenario was, quite literally, way over my head. Yet, without fully grasping the magnitude of what I faced, I was placed in charge of the mechanisms of nuclear exchange, engaging in "mutually assured destruction." "MAD" was a term used in our program, signifying the deterrence of such an exchange or forcing its uselessness to ensure that both sides would lose.

My buddies and I worked in one of the long-reaching arms of the Nuclear Triad, which consisted of three strategic platforms for launching nuclear missiles: land-based intercontinental ballistic missiles ("ICBM's"), submarines, and bombers. I was charged with the electronic interfacing of the nuclear missiles with B-52 bombers. The other aspect of my job, as a "Missile Systems Analyst," was to disassemble the parts of each missile to test and fix its radar, guidance electronics, gyros, and computer. Had I paused to reflect that the magnitude of power in one bomber loaded with nuclear weapons could equal the destructive power of two major wars combined, that thought alone might have blown a fuse in my brain. I was still a boy, entrusted with a job that countless men would shun.

The road to those moments - those crucial nanoseconds involving the very survival of humanity - was grueling. Often, in hindsight, I have thought that, had I been older and more mature, the stress may not have affected me so greatly; but, to live with what *could* have been is to give undue power to the imagination. The physical torment that I endured in my post-service days, coupled with my Nuclear-related PTSD, robbed me of the luxury of dreams. I can now only dwell in the harshness of reality.

My first taste of life in the service began in the summer of 1980. After graduating from high school and receiving a clean bill of health from my doctor in Tuscaloosa, I flew from Montgomery, Alabama to Lackland Air Force Base in San Antonio, Texas, where I withstood the rigors of twelve weeks' basic training – from intense physical exercise to my laundry duty assignment. Aside from adjusting to strict discipline (meted out in shouted commands) and acquiring such traits as steadfast dedication, orderly conduct, and alertness, the fifty new recruits and I quickly became aware of the importance of military-style conformity. From the top of our shaved heads to our leather boots, from our standard issue battle green uniforms to our dress blues, we had to look and act the same – ever alert, ever ready to comply with our drill sergeants' imperatives. Over night, freedom of choice became a thing of the past. Stripped of our individualism, we merged into a collective consciousness, with one goal: to serve our country.

Contrary to the connotation of our classification as "airmen," we had very little to do with airplanes during basic training. Instead, we were instructed in the basics of military history (with a special concentration on the Air Force) and Physical Education. The classes were generalized and much less demanding than college courses. Unlike today's basic trainees, the units of new recruits (also known as "flights") were segregated by gender, and we were not introduced to combat skills or techniques.

When, at the end of basic, our flight was evaluated on parade

drill (ceremonious maneuvering involving drilling and march-
ing), we won the distinction of Honor Flight and Honor Squadron. There were numerous flights and half as many squadrons at
Lackland at the time; so, the recognition was quite an accomplish-
ment.

At the end of October, we were processed for our next assign-
ments. By then, I had turned nineteen. Most people in my unit
were sent to training bases for various job classifications. As far as I
knew, I was the only one in my flight who did not receive a security
clearance by the end of basic training – possibly because I required
a higher degree of clearance for my training at Chanute Air Force
Base than my fellow airmen who were going to other bases. Before I left, the Air Force personnel department inquired whether I
wanted to be in the Minuteman (i.e., involving surface-to-surface
nuclear missiles) or Short Range Attack Missile ("SRAM," air-
to-ground missiles) programs. Having seen the Apollo program's
NASA moon shots, I was intrigued by ground-based rocketry, as
well as aircraft.

My destination: Chanute Air Force Base, about two hours
south of Chicago, Illinois. Decommissioned in 1993, the base
already had begun to wind down upon my arrival. Perhaps less
than five hundred men were stationed there in the early fall of
1980. Since the weather was still warm and balmy, I was assigned
to grass-cutting duty at the hospital on base before my training
classes began.

Then, in the dawn's early light, as temperatures plummeted to
below freezing levels, I marched from our barracks to our class-
rooms, in formation with fifty to sixty other airmen. Using flash-
lights, we slowly inched toward our destination, arriving in total
darkness when the batteries gave out. In hindsight, that experience
seems like a metaphor for the state of our futures – indefinable and
uncertain. Peering out of the classroom window, I could see the
barren, closed-down runway, riddled with overgrown dead weeds.

Inside the classroom, cloying steam heat kept us warm. In those rather surreal moments, Tuscaloosa seemed light years away.

Lasting about five to six hours a day, my studies were more intense than I had ever experienced in high school. The fact that I lacked proper study habits only added to the formidable challenge of exams; and the peculiar information that I had to process simply boggled my mind. Below is just a sample:

"Servo valves:

The servo valves contain a mechanical spool and a position feedback valve with a four-way flapper-nozzle fluid amplifier (figure 19), lap-spool assembly, and feedback spring. In operation, the torque motor receives a current command from the central flight system and produces a proportional torque on the diaphragm spring. The torque produces a flapper deflection which results in a differential nozzle area...."

This fairly incomprehensible verbiage was far surpassed in complexity by the workings of the missiles, themselves – though we were not encouraged to think beyond the purview of our specific jobs. These involved the testing, maintenance, and operation of missile electronics and loading target coordinates into aircraft missiles.

I dare say that that none of us had even a vague concept of nuclear war. We rarely spoke of the nuclear warheads and their functions (although later on, at my home base, we quipped about our "missile of love" and had a good laugh every time). Our concentration was on the long range B-52 and the medium range FB111 bombers. The huge scope of the SRAM program infused us with confidence in the momentous nature of our responsibilities. Being valued and feeling important infused us with a sense of purpose and impetus to continue.

During leisure time – just to get away from the training base, I gave the guys occasional rides to the city mall in my well-preserved

1979 Buick Skyhawk, watched the local kids racing their go-carts on the airstrips, frequented a small club for enlisted men, and eagerly walked to my personal mailbox (a first for me), located a quarter of a mile from my dorm. I enjoyed receiving mail from my best friend, Tom and from my mother who, by that time, had remarried and moved to Oklahoma.

After completing my training at Chanute Air Force Base, I travelled home to Tuscaloosa for a two-week stay with my family. Being away for seven months made me nostalgic for my familiar surroundings - particularly after spending my first Christmas on assignment at Chanute. The brief respite helped to renew my energies for the tasks ahead – this time at an undisclosed air force base, stateside (herein referred to as "the AFB").

In the spring of 1981, I was assigned to a bomb wing of the Munitions Maintenance squadron, which didn't have its own dormitory. Therefore, all of the married officers and others who worked on the base resided elsewhere. Without much rank and because I wasn't married, I ended up living in a squalid room in the communications dorm. The huge metal building housed more than one hundred people, all enlisted personnel. I stayed there for two years before moving into the new, more private munitions maintenance dorm, located half a mile away. These much nicer quarters were designed to house those in my unit who lived on or near the flight line, and either worked with nuclear weapons or the machines that serviced them.

At that time, the bombers had four quad, fifty caliber machine guns attached to the tail of the aircraft, and were operated by a gunner who sat in the front of the aircraft. With the bombers' jet engines wound up, ready for takeoff, a deafening sound permeated the atmosphere. Clouds of smoke rose into the air, overwhelming my olfactory senses with the smell of burning jet fuel (most likely, modern-day jet fuels do not produce as much smoke). Although, in our classified briefings, we were shown films and satellite photos of our targets, anti-aircraft sites, and Soviet naval ships, as well as the effects of nuclear blasts on other targets, the actual extent of the nuclear weapons' power defied human comprehension.

Upon approaching a bomber on the alert pad, loaded with live nuclear weapons, I experienced an adrenaline rush, which proceeded from two sources of extreme tension. One was the armed guard, carrying an M-16 rifle, standing on the alert pad, outside "the red line" encircling the bomber. The guard was tasked to monitor the analysts' strict adherence to the "two-man policy" (the ironclad rule that, when approaching a bomber with live nuclear weapons, two fellow technicians had to cross "the red line" together, carefully watching each other's hands and body motions). If either of the techs stepped out of the other's visual range or the guard interpreted any of their motions to pose a threat to the nuclear weapons, he was authorized to shoot *both* of them. In the minds of Americans, a couple of dead airmen – or, perhaps, even more – would be no price to pay for keeping the warheads safe.

The other source of heightened anxiety was, of course, the nature of what my buddies and I were doing – loading the top secret target coordinates for the end of civilization as we knew it. Depending on the way in which the bomber was configured, it could carry as many as twenty short range attack missiles. However, the configuration with which I worked had eight short range attack missiles and one large gravity bomb in the back of the bomb bay. The final bomb had a fixed strategic target, the location of which was classified. I didn't have what was called the "need to know" to access such information.[1] The first eight of these bombs had

---

1 "Need to know" is a well-known catch-phrase used by the government, particularly with regard to the military or espionage, in instances where extremely sensitive data must be restricted to the performance of one's official responsibilities. In the military, each airman receives just enough information to perform his requisite tasks – and no more. This type of access to information is designed to stave off potential sabotage and keep accidents to a minimum. "Need to know" is based on the understanding that highly sensitive information in the wrong hands is tantamount to disaster.

a yield of ten times the destructive power of the bomb dropped on Nagasaki, designed to clear a large city or comparable installation. The ninth bomb in each payload had a yield beyond the one megaton range (the actual yield was classified). The bomb was so powerful, that it had to be fitted with a Drogue Chute to slow its decent, giving the bomber time to avert the blast.

I never could wrap my head around the fact that so much potential power could be stored in such a small area.

The mission plan for the bombers at the AFB was to clear out anti-aircraft sites and to launch nuclear-tipped missiles on preliminary targets— in other words, to destroy cities the size of my hometown of Tuscaloosa or, even, Birmingham, Alabama's largest city - before delivering the final bomb to its strategic target. My job was not only interfacing the nuclear weapons with the planes, but also coding the preliminary targets in the Soviet Union, based on changing intelligence about enemy defense deployments. The warhead fit into a container not much bigger than the size of a boot box. Although, at a glance, it seemed innocuous, even getting your hands on the warhead was an indescribable experience. The vast carnage of such a nuclear disaster would overwhelm the strongest minds - that is, only those fortunate enough to live through it; but consider, would you want to survive? Robert J. Oppenheimer, the father of the atom bomb, once said, "In some sort of crude sense, which no vulgarity, no humor, no overstatement can quite extinguish, the physicists have known sin; and this is knowledge which they cannot lose." Those with knowledge understand the cruel human need for hegemony – the will to dominate. At a very young age, my buddy and I were privy to information that was extremely difficult to comprehend – let alone to bear - with lives hinging on our every move; but we had no choice. We did what we had to do. There was no time for reflection or probing. Now, as I write and ponder, the memories remain with me still. I am wracked by stress, a consequence of the awareness that I cannot lose.

Working on the flight line, I calibrated the missiles' guidance systems and ran missile launch simulations. I was also responsible for extracting a bomber missile's Flight Information Recorder Transcript (the "FIRT"), which contained a detailed mission on in-flight testing and showed the bomber's launching capability.

When the B-52's landed and were parked, we hooked up power to the bomber, ran our tests, and extracted the FIRT. We jumped on the plane so fast, that the ground crew rarely had time to put the safety pins in the ejection seats. Therefore, when performing tests, the analysts had to sit in the unpinned seats (which were powered by a small rocket). Without employing enormous vigilance, a technician could lose his life by inadvertently activating the ejection seat, causing it to hit the tarmac and bounce back up into the airman, killing him. Although these tragic accidents did occur, they were extremely rare.

Danger, however, was never really avoidable. It was a way of life. Occasionally, when the Inspector General would visit the base, I was awakened at 3:00 a.m. by a loud pounding on my door, and was informed that the President of the United States had given the order to launch a nuclear strike against the Soviet Union. Jumping out of bed and into my private car, I raced to a hangar, where my buddy and I climbed into a government vehicle and sped to the alert pad. Before crossing "the red line," we produced our security clearance at checkpoints manned by the military police armed with M-16's. Then, the aircrew handed us a tape that had to be put on a reel-to-reel machine. Once we hooked that up to the bomber's missile computer, we loaded the top secret target coordinates – longitude, latitude, and elevation for the detonation of each missile. Then, both of us moved to the hatch. One of us watched, as the other jumped inside the bomber to ensure that the computer took all of the coordinates (this was known as "the target checkpoint"). When we verified that all of the coordinates were there and in place, we exited the plane as fast as we could, so that the crew could board and start taxiing down the runway. Unbeknownst to us, the Doomsday Clock was at three and four minutes to midnight. Due to the pervasive, extremely high tension, I (and, possibly, some of the others) performed in somewhat of a panic mode, in a race toward the end of civilization. Until we had evidence to the contrary, this was the real thing!

In those targeted cities and towns, hundreds of thousands – perhaps, even millions – slept, worked, lived, and breathed - oblivious to the unspeakable carnage that was to be meted upon them – or would it? When would it come, and how many lives would be lost?

When we got out of the bomber, the aircrew jumped in and closed the hatch. The pilots powered up the bombers' eight engines, and rolled out to the end of the flight line. Once in position for takeoff, they revved up the engines to the maximum rpm,[2] and looked at their orders. Was this the real thing, or just a drill - a rehearsal for the end of time?[3] If, while the engines were still wound up and the pilots let off the brakes, that very well could have been it – the end of civilization as we knew it; but, when they dropped the rpm to idle, we knew that it was just a drill. Looking on, I watched, petrified and practically motionless, like a stone statue.

If, in fact, the United States launched a nuclear strike (whether offensive or defensive in nature), it most likely would not be lim-

---

2 "rpm" means revolutions per minute.

3 It is important to note here that, for decades, U.S. military aircraft have not flown with live nuclear weapons on patrols or on practice missions, due to aircraft crashes that spread live warheads and/or radioactive material across large areas. However, in 2007, live nuclear-tipped missiles were flown from Minot Air Force Base to the AFB, where they remained loaded on a bomber thirty-six-hours, during which time the weapons remained unprotected, and were not reported missing. Referred to by observers as a "Bent Spear incident," it involved a nuclear weapon event of significant concern, but without the threat of nuclear war. The incident necessitated a significant reorganization in the Air Force, and led to the creation of the Air Force Global Strike Command to monitor and control all United States Air Force nuclear warheads and employees.

ited and, certainly, would initiate a reciprocal action by the Soviet Union in the form of extremely high-altitude ICBM's (reaching fifteen-thousand miles an hour at the edge of space) that would release "MIRV's"[4] on the United States. The AFB would have been a prime target. The power of the warheads was so staggering, and the destruction so complete, that taking shelter after the bombers' launch would be useless. Though not a foregone conclusion, Armageddon became all too real in those moments.

It was all far too much for a boy of nineteen, who barely had explored life in all of its dimensions – charged (as life should be for anyone of that age) with the illusion of immortality. If I allow my mind to journey back to the past, I find myself there again - in the early dawn of my youth – facing the potential destruction of our planet. The finality of my purpose was terrifying, but I dared not think the unthinkable. I simply couldn't, for I had no idea where to begin.

---

4 A multiple independently targeted reentry vehicle ("MIRV") warhead is a collection of nuclear weapons that are carried on a single intercontinental ballistic missile ("ICBM") or a submarine-launched ballistic missile ("SLBM") that can strike several targets individually or fewer targets repeatedly.

Chapter 3
24/7 Alert

From my perspective, the world is a dangerous place. If you spent a significant part of your life working with machinery capable of annihilating humanity, you would, no doubt, feel the same. It's hard for me to envision or imagine a circumstance in which I would not feel a heightened sense of the world around me - in tune and hypervigilant in every situation. Even today, so-called "normal," everyday experiences assume a momentous character for me, causing sensations that precisely mirror my original trauma of working with weapons of mass destruction. My startle responses cause me to do, sense, and feel things that others would, perhaps, ignore. For example, a simple bump on the head causes most people to draw back with an "Ouch!" I, on the other hand, endure one strike, followed by an intense startle reaction which, in turn, causes a repetition of that motion, due to lightening-fast reflexes. The pain doubles, and so does the trauma. Every day, in one way or another, I am at war – in hand-to-hand combat with my nerves.

While at the AFB I had several significant experiences, which resurface in my everyday reality and create dangerous scenarios in my world – even where none exist. This is not to say that my imagination is at play. On the contrary, that which I feel and experience is very real. The stimuli around me exist. I am, simply, hypersensitive to them. These extrinsic stimuli in my personal purview take me back in time, and I am there again, on the cusp of potential global disaster.

One particularly memorable incident surfaces in my mind. One night, my buddy Danny whom I met at the Chanute training base, and I were playing a game of ping pong in an office in our hanger. Suddenly, the phone rang. Someone else took the call and, then, precipitously gave us an order to go out to a bomber, situ-

20

ated well beyond the alert pad. Hurriedly, we grabbed our tool box, hardly knowing what to expect.

As Danny and I crossed the temporary two-man policy boundary, we noticed countless emergency vehicles and officers ("brass") surrounding a bomber, as flashing emergency lights illuminated the darkness around us. As we approached the bomb bay to determine what the problem was, we discovered that one of the live nuclear missiles was stuck in the armed position. Moving quickly and with intense resolve, we didn't stop to contemplate what we faced. Looking through a clear glass window, we observed a red "A." Reaching in, we attempted to manipulate the switch with a special tool, similar to a screw driver. When this procedure failed, we proceeded to tap on the tool with a hammer. I felt extremely uneasy, but dared not give vent to the feeling. Whenever the term "nuclear" is injected into the equation, an entirely new and escalated sense of purpose, danger, and forced courage come into play. Like others in our position, Danny and I were on autopilot, knowing that it was best not to think too much – especially about the possible (though highly unlikely) event that the motor could fire, causing a conflagration, and spreading radioactive material across a wide path.

Eventually, we successfully safed the missile, and quietly resumed our normal states of breathing. We spoke not a word to each other about the incident afterward. We knew what we were doing, and we simply executed our jobs. Words were superfluous. Our stress level was already so high, that feeling on edge was a given – a natural consequence of being there.

Due to the extremely sensitive nature of the job, easygoing friendships were hampered on base (except for my association with Danny and Phillip, one of my supervisors for whom I cut grass off base). My existence was perpetually guarded, and I was constantly aware of being monitored and, possibly, followed. Keenly in tune with my environment, I remained in a state of 24/7 hypervigilant alert.

One night (most likely, on a weekend), I drove off base into town to find something to do. Upon my return, I noticed a car behind me. At first, I didn't think much about it; however, when I looked through the rearview mirror several minutes later, I saw the same car. With my senses in high gear, I began to make random turns, as the car continued to follow me. After making a couple of more haphazard turns, the vehicle continued to pursue me all the way down a road that dead-ended at the base. When the car reached a half-way point down that path, it made a U-turn, right in the middle of the road, and veered in the opposite direction. It's just the Office of Special Investigations ("the OSI"), doing its job, I thought to myself - either that or I had attracted too much attention to myself by driving a nice new car that was not easily affordable on an airman's pay.

On another off-duty occasion, a stranger approach me and asked how many bombers were on our base. Observing my guarded demeanor, the man let the conversation drop. I never knew whether I was confronting a casual interlocutor or a KGB agent, trying to assess my behavior or obtain classified information. In all events, I felt that I had to be in control of myself and my environment at all times – aware of every syllable that I uttered and every move that I made.

As time passed, I became increasingly tired of living in a state of animated suspension. The overwhelming stress made me more than eager to return to civilian life, and I began to prepare for that eventuality. To that end, I put money in the GI Bill, so that I could attend college upon my discharge. That day came in late July, 1984, when I was almost twenty-three. The joy that I felt in my new-found freedom had no bounds. My duty in the service ended just as it had begun – precipitously and without any fanfare or logical transition. I just went from one world – a universe charged with reactivity, to living the days of my youth – much of which had been irretrievably lost. I never even stopped to take off my uniform. I simply drove home, without any instruction or preparation for my old/new life. I never got a debriefing at any time. Later, I felt as though this put me at a disadvantage. I believe that, had I been given a debriefing, in the same manner as combat troops, my re-initiation into civilian life would have gone more smoothly.

All at once, the future lay before me, and I went through the motions of learning how to navigate in the world again. Nothing seemed to have changed – except me, that is. I was extremely uptight and could never relax. I didn't know it then, but I was, of course, repressing thoughts of my traumatic days at the AFB, my "home base." Feelings and emotions about my days of living on the brink of disaster followed me like shadows, swarming the latent recesses of my unconscious mind. I was still hypervigilant, succumbing to the pent-up emotions that I dared not acknowledge in my moments of terror. Yet, I didn't know what was happening to me – that, in fact, I was suffering from Post Traumatic Stress Disorder (PTSD). It took me many years to discover that truth.

In those early days after being discharged, however, I didn't want to contemplate much more than starting over. By all appearances, I got my wish. My job at the grocery store was still waiting for me, and I received my salary and raises as though I had never left (which was the legal trend at the time). Having moved in with my father, I voluntarily paid him $200 a month for rent. Gradually, I began to integrate into society again – but with painstaking effort. My friend Tommy and I went to dance clubs, and I attempted to socialize and date. Somehow, though, the fact that I wasn't able to relax completely had a noticeable effect on my relationships with women. My entire persona was still tied up in knots, on 24/7 alert - waiting for that all important call, the next crisis, the next potential order to launch.

Yet, after being four years behind on my life, I was inhaling Tuscaloosa air again. I was back where I once belonged, and life seemed to resume a normal character. Smoldering beneath the surface, however, was an internal battle, the likes of which I just couldn't describe or pinpoint - one which I most definitely was not ready to face.

Chapter 4
Superman In Training

*M*y time in the service taught me, early on, that life doesn't come with an instruction handbook. In every given instance, you just have to do the best that you can, go with your gut, and move on. For me, "moving on" meant going to college and enhancing my skills to equip me for civilian life. As I mentioned, I contributed to the GI Bill and was able to pursue my studies. Initially, however, the government informed me that it lacked evidence of my payment. So, I conducted a search, and found most of the cancelled checks, except for two or three. Because the latter were lost, as much as three times the value of these checks (nearly $1,500 to $2,000) was not deposited into my GI bill fund. The government was responsible for keeping track of those funds, but it lost all of documentation indicating that I had participated in the GI bill program. Therefore, a little ingenuity on my part went a long way. Had I not found the cancelled checks, I never could have afforded an advanced education.

Eager to be productive and reintegrate into society, I attended the University of Alabama and chose an Arts and Sciences curriculum. I sent out resumes, and was first offered a job with a company as a quality assurance ("QA") inspector with Rockwell International missile systems in Georgia. Although I was more than qualified for the position, we could not reach a salary agreement. Not long afterward, BF Goodrich (herein referred to as "the Plant") where my father worked as an accountant, put out an advisory notice about available jobs. I went for an interview, and was hired as a QA inspector, performing light duty – checking tolerances on tires and machinery, ensuring that the finished product functioned well, and that the tires were properly labeled. I then recorded my findings on paper, which I turned in at the end of my shift. The

Plant was located at the very site that I viewed from my front yard as a child. Life had come eerily full-circle.

During this period, my undiagnosed PTSD was a fact of life, but I still couldn't label it. However, I knew that something was awry. Although my social life was greatly affected, I happened to meet a girl (to whom I will refer as "Joan") at the beach in the summer of 1988. We struck up a friendship and, soon, began dating. An RN at a local hospital, Joan was fun and interesting. We went to the beach, jet skiing, and even did some traveling together. I was intrigued by her profession, especially since I always loved assisting people. One day, I accompanied her to the cardiac care unit, where she was tending to a postoperative male patient. When the man saw me, he reached out and squeezed my finger, signifying that he was in pain. In that moment, I knew that, someday, I wanted to attend nursing school and positively impact people's lives.

While keeping that aspiration in view, I had to earn a living and attend to my duties at the Plant. About three and a half years into the job, the company downsized and reassigned thirteen QA employees to production jobs, which involved heavy labor. I was relegated to a second-step tire builder's position. Not even a year went by before I injured my back while pulling and manipulating a tire in order to position it onto the building machinery. Initially, I experienced sharp back pain, which immediately became a progressively worsening condition, which never subsided during my time at the Plant. I reported my injury to the Plant's nurse's office and, subsequently, documented several injuries there over a period of weeks. Unbeknownst to me at first, one of the injuries to the top of my foot was caused by a pinched nerve in my back that radiated into that area.

Enter Dr. Phillip K. Bobo, the Plant's doctor at the time, who examined me at the dispensary. I had every reason to trust him, since I had heard that he was a good doctor with a well-established reputation in the ER. In spite of his apparent competence, I was struck by his smugness and penchant to avert my glance. He simply didn't look me in the eye, and never addressed me. He only spoke to whomever else was with him in the room. Despite my discomfort, I wanted to gain insight into the nature of my condition. Dr. Bobo recommended that ice be applied on my back (and, possibly, some over-the-counter medication), and suggested that I resume my job in production. My work involved constant twisting, handling, and pushing four to six tons on the floor during each shift – hardly appropriate tasks for someone with my level of pain intensity.

Dr. Bobo's recommendation contradicted the express advice of my personal orthopedist, Dr. Blair Behringer, M.D., from whom I obtained a second opinion. In a letter to Dr. Bobo dated November 22, 1989, Dr. Behringer diagnosed me with grade one spondylolisthesis, a condition in which a vertebra in the lower spine (typically the fifth lumbar vertebra) slips forward on the sacrum. When slippage is significant, it may cause nerve compression. Dr. Behringer's correspondence stated further, in pertinent part:

"[Greg Hardin], with a grade one spondylolithesis, is at risk for back difficulties with a heavy laboring job and it would be prudent (emphasis added) *for him to be assigned to somewhat lighter work with that problem in mind."* The letter went on to state, *"However, his current situation in terms of physical capacity does not preclude[5] his performing his current duties."* In other words, although I was technically capable of resuming my heavy labor position, (I had full range of motion at that time, specifically noted and documented by Dr. Behringer), I clearly was at risk in doing so. Therefore, Dr. Behringer called for "prudence" on Dr. Bobo's part in reassigning me to lighter work. This language merited particular scrutiny, since it required that Dr. Bobo exercise caution and circumspection with regard to the job risks that I faced.

Throwing caution to the wind, however, Dr. Bobo chose to act in the best interest of the Plant, instead of my own. As a result,

---

5 Note: The word "preclude" here means to foreclose or make impossible.

once the initial back injury occurred, difficulties arose during every shift, after which I found myself in the nurse's office each night. At first, I lay down on an ice pack under my back. Soon, however, my back became so tender, that I felt as though I were lying on a pipe (which was, in fact, my spine!). I then had to turn over onto my stomach with the ice on my back. Such changes were never noted in the nurse's reports and, for most of the time, I was in the dark about what was going on. I erroneously assumed that I could rely upon healthcare professionals – ultimately to enlighten me and ensure my welfare. Sadly, however, such was not the case. The sharp pain in my back would make any mortal man recoil. I, however, had been exposed to situations in the air force that defied description. Innately, therefore, I felt that, due to my military discipline and experiences in the service, I could withstand inordinate pain with superhuman strength. With each instance of shooting pain, and due to my extreme tenderness and instability in that area, therefore, I mustered my inner strength, grit my teeth, and lay there for fifteen minutes virtually every shift (as per Dr. Bobo's instructions). I remained cold and still – as though I were Superman in training.

Without a diagnosis of PTSD, I was at a loss as to how to remedy or, even, acknowledge it. Significantly, the concurrence of chronic pain and PTSD has been referred to as "mutual maintenance." That is, the presence of both exacerbates the symptoms of either. It is still inconceivable to me, therefore, that I was cleared to pursue a job that inevitably would cause the onset of persistent distress.

At some point, an RN on duty approached me with my pre-employment spine x-ray report that had been in the company's possession. "Don't tell anyone that I gave this to you," she admonished me. On November 27, 1989, the pain in my back had escalated to such an intensity, that I had to go to the ER that night after work. The report showed my spine's condition to be a "class C," and indicated the presence of "congenital [i.e. birth] defects…of the L5 vertebral body" (the prerequisite for employment at the Plant was a class "B" or better since, according to industrial classifications, a "class C" is a no-hire x-ray). The report expressly indicated that Dr. Bobo was the attending physician (although he did not see me on that occasion). These findings contradicted the company's former physician, who labeled his report "class B, OK to work." The report was initialed by an RN who, ostensibly, was authorized to sign off on it. As the attending physician, Dr. Bobo had access to this assessment but, nonetheless, authorized me to return to work, as usual. Obviously, the Plant had preexisting awareness of my congenital spine defects, which the nurse clandestinely revealed to me. In effect, the company knowingly hired me with a class "C" ("no-hire") x-ray. However, without a medical degree, I had very little understanding of the documents' meaning and content. I might as well have been reading Mandarin Chinese. By flagrantly dismissing his obligation to reveal the truth and reassign me to lighter duty, Dr. Bobo breached his Hippocratic Oath to "first do no harm." If I had known of my birth defect, I never would have been doing heavy labor!

The culpable parties, therefore, were the Plant and Dr. Bobo. Had the company exercised due care and paid heed to my x-ray, I would have been fine (I can't think of any other job for which I potentially could have been hired that would even have approximated the level of heavy labor required at the Plant). Unfortunately, however, except for paying me two days' workers' compensation, the Plant refused to assist me on all counts.

Bewildered, I appealed twice to the Plant's personnel office, and both times, Bob H., who met me at the counter, informed me, "Mr. Hardin, we are not going to help you with a preexisting condition." The cat was out of the bag – at the eleventh hour, and the wool was painfully pulled from my eyes. No clichés in the world could rectify the injustices meted upon me. My next step, therefore, was to prevail upon the legal system to regress the gross negligence[6] that was perpetrated against me.

In 1990, I was released from the Plant, with my once promising future in jeopardy. Going forward with my life was an exercise in becoming Superman - taking on the world emotionally and physically – and little knowing what was in store.

---

6 An act undertaken with conscious, voluntary disregard of the use of reasonable care, which results in foreseeable injury.

ĹM A. ASKEW, M.D., P.C.
ŃRY HOLLINGSWORTH, M.D.
ĹIAM C. FINLAY, M.D.
ŃRY NELSON, M.D.
ĹLIAM A. BRIGHT, M.D.

X-RAY REPORT

THE RADIOLOGY CLINIC

427 UNIVERSITY BLVD., EAST
TUSCALOOSA, ALABAMA 35401

RONALD C. PHELPS, M.D.
JOHN G. KAHLER, M.D.
R. MARK KENDRICK, M.D.
TIMOTHY L. McGHEE, M.D.
CHARLES E. KING, JR., M.D.

NAME_____Harden, Gregory   23467_____ AGE__24wm_ X-RAY NO._86-51__

ADDRESS_____ DATE_1-3-86_____

REFERRED BY:

Dr. Sawyer
Ecare

FINDINGS

CHEST:

The heart and lungs are normal.

CONCLUSION:

Chest within normal limits.

LUMBAR SPINE:

There is some irregularity of the epiphyseal plates thought due
to the developmental origin. There is also narrowing of the
fifth lumbar interspace with some forward displacement of
L5 on S1 compatible with spondylolisthesis, Stage I.

CONCLUSION:

1. Minor congenital anomaly of the epiphyseal plates.
2. Stage I spondylolisthesis at the lumbosacral level.
Class C.

Class C - okay to work
Dr. Bullard A++R

W. Askew md

WAA/mm

_____
RADIOLOGIST
W.A. Askew, M. D.

ORTHOPAEDIC AND
REHABILITATION
ASSOCIATES, P.C.

BLAIR R. BEHRINGER, M.D., F.A.C.S.

November 22, 1989

Dr. Phillip Bobo
32 15th Street East
Tuscaloosa, Alabama 35401

re: Greg Hardin

Dear Dr. Bobo:

In response to your request for my assessment of the current
situation of Greg Hardin. The following information is provided.
Please note that I have enclosed a copy of both of my chart notes on
this patient.

Mr. Hardin has grade I spondylolythesis which has not changed since
pre-employment films dated 1/3/86. Specifically, I can see no
change in his x-rays over a period of time of approximately three
years.

He, with a grade one spondylolythesis is at risk for back difficulties
with a heavy laboring job and it would be prudent for him to be
assigned to somewhat lighter work with that problem in mind.
However his current situation in terms of physical capacity does not
preclude his performing his current duties.

Sincerely yours,

Blair R. Behringer, M.D.

13

11/09/89

Greg Hardin

Greg is a very pleasant 29 year old man who is a tire builder at Goodrich. He has had intermittent "muscle pulls" on a fairly frequent basis and was seen last Friday. X-rays revealed a suspicion of spondylolysis and he was referred here for an evaluation.

On examination Greg has a essentially full range of motion and normal strength about his back and all joint of the upper and lower extremities bilaterally. He has mild lumbo-sacral discomfort.

X-rays reveal bilateral spondylolysis and a grade one slip.

Impression: As above.
BRB/kwe

Chapter 5
The Duel

*I*n light of what I had been through in my young life, it was no wonder that I experienced a great deal of disillusionment. Inherently, I realized that I had witnessed far too much for one of my age; and, without proper guidance as to how to deal with all of my emotions and reactions (these had a label: PTSD – I just didn't know it yet), I felt directionless and, in a very real sense, betrayed. For four years, I had served my country and risked my life for what I thought was the greater good. I should have been proud – and I was; but something just wasn't right, and I couldn't pinpoint the cause of my distress. I felt detached from the world, isolated and alone – even when I was with people - constantly in a state of hyperawareness. My startle responses were very exaggerated. Sudden noises would send me into ready-to-launch mode. To compound matters, my body was a receptacle of pain, the result of which was the negligence of Dr. Bobo and others, who purportedly possessed medical expertise and knowledge. Why was I released to engage in a heavy labor job with a class "C" x-ray? Worse, why did those with knowledge of my preexisting birth defect employ me in the first place, and why was this vital information kept from me? Were it not for the nurse who secretly disclosed my report, I would have been completely in the dark. I knew that I had to get to the heart of the matter – my life and my future; but, first, I had to address the injustices that had befallen me.

Soon after leaving the Plant in 1990, I decided to seek legal representation. The first person who came to mind was my relative, Ron, an attorney in town, whom I had every reason to trust. Upon evaluating my case, Ron agreed to pursue a personal injury cause of action against the Plant and a possible suit against Dr. Bobo. In furtherance of the discovery process, I met with Ron regularly, apprising him of my medical history, courses of treatment and any physical problems that arose over time. At that point, I experienced a low to medium level of constant pain, accompanied by occasional sharp, debilitating, shooting pains in my lower back, caused by pinched nerves. When moving, I had to employ good body mechanics, so as to avoid exacerbation of the condition. Despite my physical pain, I took some comfort in the notion that the legal system would redress my well-held grievances.

As I struggled with physical discomfort, I also withstood daily escalating (and, as yet, undiagnosed) PTSD symptoms. I was still a college student, taking a part-time load, desperately trying to integrate social activities into my daily routine. The PTSD was becoming so acute, however, that I began to withdraw and become more hypervigilant. Dancing, one of my favorite pastimes, became a thing of history, due to my back injury, and any loud music would, most certainly, act as a trigger that catapulted me into hyperawareness. I noticed that certain activities, however (such as jet skiing, for example), decreased my back pain. Dr. Behringer later informed me that the motor's vibration actually caused a decrease in my pain level; but the nature of jet skiing, generally, damaged my back, and was just too much for me. So, after two rides on the lake, I ceased the activity entirely.

Eventually, due to exacerbated PTSD (which made even little confrontations seem momentous), my girlfriend Joan and I parted. Some time later, inspired by my experience that day with the cardiac patient in Joan's care, I decided to attend nursing classes. The question was, how could I fulfill that goal when so many unfathomable ever-worsening sensations (e.g., intense stress, worsening depression, poor concentration, apathy, emotional rage, anxiety, startle reflex, and other similar symptoms) were overtaking me? In other words, how could I integrate into a world from which I felt so alienated? Without a full understanding of my condition (not to mention the lack of proper medical treatment), I found myself constantly en garde, as if I were in a duel with an unnamed antagonist, taking one step forward and two steps back, in a perpetual state of self-defense.

In trying to decipher the source of my undiagnosed PTSD, the thought occurred to me that the SRAM on which my buddy, Danny and I had worked while at the AFB had the potential to burn or detonate during an accident or fire, dispersing radioactive material over a wide area. Of course, at the time of the incident, I had no knowledge of this fact; however, it may very well have been a major cause for the development of PTSD in my case - and others,' for that matter. For that very reason, the Department of Defense subsequently removed the SRAM from the nuclear arsenal. To think that Danny and I had been beating on it to safe the missile! It is, therefore, logical to conclude that the traumatic event was a PTSD trigger.

My physical distress, occasioned by long periods of sitting and studying required in nursing school, placed even more stress on my back. My ability to focus was severely impaired, and I worried about my exam performance. At times, my back pain became so intense, that I had to stand in the back of the class. I'm certain that the other students noticed my rather unusual behavior – but others' impressions of me were immaterial. I just wanted to feel centered and well again; but that wish was confined to the realm of my mind, alone.

Despite insurmountable obstacles, I managed to take and pass my exams and begin working as a part-time operating room nurse. Amazingly, I succeeded in getting through nursing school and working part-time in the operating room without lifting any patients. Because I was always wary about that aspect of my job, I took care to avoid it at all cost. Unfortunately, my PTSD and back injury symptoms further increased during this period, and affected the quality of my work. Functioning in my daily life became ever more difficult (an apt analogy would be constantly trying to text while driving). I had begun to experience hyperhidrosis (i.e., excessive perspiration), "fight or flight" syndrome, and intense distraction. Whenever the operating room's phone rang unexpectedly, my PTSD was triggered to the Nth degree. That sound, reverberating throughout the O.R., reminded me of "the call" to load target coordinates to launch! With my past recurring before my eyes at any given moment, I felt displaced in my environment - a victim of my internal war of nerves.

Upon visiting my orthopedist, Dr. Behringer, again in 1991, I was evaluated for a range of motion rating. So that existing deficits could be observed and noted, I had to wait for maximum healing from my injuries incurred at the Plant. Tests revealed that I had an eighteen percent impairment rating, which indicated some level of disability. To go from full range of motion to that level of incapacity and pain was significant. Through all of the confusion and bewilderment, I knew that, for my lawsuit to succeed, I required proof of my level of physical capacity prior and subsequent to my back injury. I therefore requested that Dr. Behringer's daughter (who worked in his office at the time) provide me with my medical reports. Her response was astounding. "All of your records burned in a fire, Mr. Hardin," she informed me, helpless to rectify the matter. This *cannot* be happening, I thought to myself. Thankfully, I had the report which revealed the eighteen percent range of motion impairment, along with other medical documentation to corroborate my condition and, ultimately, validate my cause of action against the Plant and Dr. Bobo.

At around this time, Kenneth Walters, then Vice President of the local Rubber Workers Union, confidentially informed me that, after my release, the Plant ceased to hire employees with class "C" spine x-rays.[7] After he retired, he proceeded to give me the names of those who, due to no-hire x-rays, were denied employment. The significant alteration in customary hiring practices evidenced

---

7 Subsequent to his promotion to president of the union, Mr. Walters gave express consent to the use of his name in this narrative. He has since retired.

the Plant's awareness that something had gone terribly wrong in my case, warranting a change in protocol. While this avoidance of future recurrences of negligence further bolstered my case, it could not take away from the fact that I was injured and without recourse.

As my symptoms worsened, I tried such self-help measures as pain clinics, chiropractic, swimming, and several other treatment modalities, all of which did not have long-term, sustainable benefits. Bending, stooping, and twisting motions became increasingly painful. By the time I graduated from nursing school in 1992, my back pain had escalated. This was due to the fact that for the first time since leaving the Plant, I was trying to work full time. As a result of my intense physical discomfort, I worked as a nurse only for a matter of weeks before realizing that surgery was my sole remaining option. More than I ever could have imagined, I was at the mercy of an unknown enemy, fighting a relentless duel.

Chapter 6
Time Out

*T*o most people, the mere notion of surgery is daunting – and I can't say that I relished the thought, myself; but, in the interest of maintaining quality of life, I decided to go ahead with it, feeling that, eventually, my pain would diminish. At the very least, I expected that the operation would enable me to exert myself physically, without feeling incapacitated. My constant pain was caused by instability of the fifth vertebra; and, with just a small amount of exertion, sudden sharp, debilitating nerve impingements pervaded the area. When I wasn't beset by pinched nerves, that region still remained tender, due to the vertebra's instability, which necessitated surgical intervention (i.e., anchoring). My labor-intensive work at the Plant triggered these injuries and exacerbated my preexisting birth defect (of which I was still unaware).

Naturally, at age thirty-one, with my entire future still ahead of me, I wanted to look forward to as much productivity as possible. With my RN degree, I was eager to reach out and help those in more dire situations than I. I had always been – and still remain – empathetic to the plights of others, recognizing the larger – more global - experience of which all of us are a part. Yet, to some degree, my back pain and spine instability, coupled with my undiagnosed/untreated PTSD, left me feeling emotionally vulnerable and obscured my vision of moving on.

In the days leading up to my surgery, therefore, I felt a kind of emotional numbness – detachment from the world - that I just couldn't explain. I was an island, struggling to stay afloat - in a perpetual time-out period that no one (not even I) – could explain. Never, in those moments, could I have imagined that, as time passed, my feelings of emotional ambivalence and alienation would further increase - to a shocking degree. My inner turmoil caused a communication rift with my family and, consequently, I had little support

41

going into the operation. Nonetheless, the surgery at least afforded me an opportunity to feel better, and I jumped at the chance.

Given my medical knowledge, I expected some postoperative pain. I also realized that, due to the spinal fusion, my range of motion would decrease. With support braces and pedicle screws (used to anchor the spine) in my back, fluid movement was virtually impossible. However, I was unprepared for the level of discomfort that I experienced. I felt as though I were entrapped in my body – physically and emotionally, struggling at every moment with symptoms that I could not define. The first time I got up to walk with the nurses, I felt an incredible pain in my spine; but I told myself that the escalated discomfort would, in time, go away.

For about a year, my life was on hold. I took time off from work and tried to resume my daily routine at home. I was living alone and, since I was not in close contact with family, I had to fend for myself when attempting to run errands and engaging in other basic activities. About a week after the surgery, however, my mother came into town to help out. To say the least, recovery time was rough. Mom cooked and cleaned for me, and even assisted with basic personal hygiene. In order to wash my hair, for example, I had to lie down with my head over the edge of my bed, while Mom did the honors.

Although I was relieved and grateful for Mom's presence, no amount of assistance could ameliorate my gnawing physical distress. Incredibly, I ultimately sought intervention from pain clinics! What was going on? I wondered. I understood that a little pain after surgery was to be expected, but I quickly realized that my discomfort exceeded the anticipated level, and all attempts to alleviate the pain provided limited, temporary relief, at best. My physical difficulties (especially sitting for long periods) only became more acute as the days passed.

To compound matters, my medical bills (prior and subsequent to the surgery) continued to mount. As time went on, I tried to find a job as an RN, but I knew that my disability would impede my performance level. Prior to my back injury, I had been extremely motivated and strong, always relying on my physical prowess, which enabled me to lead a productive life. One can only imagine the overwhelming paradigm shift that I experienced!

Meanwhile, matters regarding my personal injury (and potential malpractice) case(s) were proceeding much too slowly. As I mentioned, I had every reason to place my faith in Ron, but my suit seemed to be inert - in a kind of holding pattern. Becoming suspicious and impatient, I decided to consult with another attorney in Birmingham. Unbelievably, that attorney told me that Ron had allowed the statute of limitations to run out on the case that could have been filed against the Plant, my former employer. From the inception of our attorney-client relationship, whenever I expressed concern about potential time limitations on my suit, Ron assured me that I shouldn't be concerned. Clearly, he equivocated, fabricated, and strung me along. In hindsight, I considered that, perhaps, he didn't realize the level of my distress. Just by looking at me, he probably couldn't discern the extent to which I suffered – physically and emotionally. As a superman in training, I unintentionally masked pain that often defied ordinary human tolerance. Due to my undiagnosed PTSD, coupled with the fact that I had been trained to function calmly under stress, I, myself, didn't consciously fathom the degree to which I suffered in silence.

Inside, I waged a very private battle. Upon hearing the news about Ron, I began to cry. That was the straw that broke the camel's back (let alone mine). As my stress level incrementally escalated, I experienced an increase in physical pain. It is important to note, however, that there was no direct causal relationship between the two trigger factors (i.e., my undiagnosed PTSD and pain). In other words, although the undiagnosed PTSD and the pain occurred simultaneously, each was independent of the other.

Realizing that I had to rectify my emotional and physical time out, I couldn't even begin to wallow in self-pity. Most significantly, the undiagnosed PTSD kept me in active survival mode. So, with my brain running a mile a minute, I picked up the phone and reported Ron to the Alabama State Bar Association. I then began to seek advice from other attorneys, with a view to prosecuting my relative, Ron, for malpractice. Betrayal. That was all I could think about. When I couldn't find anyone to take my case against Ron, I went to the state bar and testified as to his actions and omissions.

Although I'm not at liberty to speak of the proceedings, the Bar informed me that, in fact, Ron had mishandled my case. Acknowledging that fact, the Bar broke protocol and issued a letter to a local attorney on my behalf, requesting representation in my possible legal malpractice case. Predictably, upon being informed of the potential charges against him, Ron denied liability. He stated further that he didn't have malpractice insurance and that, even if he did, he wouldn't pay a penny.

That was it. The lawyer who, purportedly, had been on my side didn't want to hear another word. Apparently, attorneys in the state of Alabama are not required to have malpractice insurance. Given that impediment, the statute timed out as to Ron, as well. Without further recourse, I took matters into my own hands, and decided to obtain a parade permit from local police and picket in front of the Plant, Ron's law office, and Dr. Bobo's Emergicare center. PTSD vets have a strong sense of justice, and I was not going to stand by and allow history to repeat itself. What happened to me must never recur, I told myself. Although I was unaware of the fact, I was also a disabled veteran with PTSD, who had placed my life at risk for our collective freedoms. The question was, "Why were my personal liberties being so unfairly compromised?"

Armed with incriminating signs, I alternated my picketing activities between the Plant, Ron's and Dr. Bobo's offices. Depending upon how I felt, I picketed on and off for a week at a time at all three places. I also reported Dr. Bobo to Mr. D. at the Board of

Medical Examiners who, after a brief investigation, claimed that Dr. Bobo was not liable for any wrongdoing. In the same breath, he tellingly added, "Dr. Bobo is a friend of mine, and we are not going to discipline him." "If he didn't do anything wrong," I retorted, in disbelief, "why am I standing outside Emergicare, holding a sign?" I am a sensible person, never given to wrathful displays – except in instances when I am unjustly treated. I didn't need the extra stress, which only served to exacerbate my undiagnosed PTSD and escalating back pain. Such facts begged the question: if my grievances were not viable, why would I have wasted my time?

Although I had missed my chance to pursue legal action against the wrongdoers (including Ron - the very person whom I trusted as an ally), I wanted to do everything in my power to prevent justice from ultimately timing out. Principle, alone, was the motivating factor for me; so, despite my physical discomfort and emotional anguish, I continued to let my voice be heard. In the process, I made a surprising discovery. As I stood in the median outside of Ron's office, I observed him moving items out into his car. Pausing briefly to wonder what was happening, I quickly resumed picketing. Then, as Ron approached, threatening and harassing me, I flagged someone down with a cell phone and called the police. When law enforcement arrived, a few choice words were used to keep Ron at bay, connoting "If you don't desist, you'll be in trouble."

That incident marked my final week of protest in front of Ron's law office. Unbeknownst to me, during that very week, the Alabama State Bar had suspended his law license. While it is unclear as to whether his conduct in my case was directly related to his suspension, I believe that it was, at least, one contributing factor. Evidently, Ron had a history of unprofessional conduct, which one local (1997) newspaper described as "…likely to cause immediate and serious injury to a client or to the public." Although to some degree, I felt relieved, my problems were far from over - and still had not been justly redressed.

As I resorted more and more to self-help, I reached out to various state and federal agencies, including the Department of Labor, the Alabama Governor's office and the President of the United States. No one was listening. All the while, life was dealing me yet another unpredictable hand – and the joker was smiling.

Local lawyer suspended

■ **MONTGOMERY** — Tuscaloosa attorney ▓▓▓▓ has been temporarily suspended from practicing law, according to an announcement from the Disciplinary Commission of the Alabama State Bar.

The disciplinary board took the action March 27.

"Based on information provided, the Disciplinary Commission concluded ▓▓▓▓ **Local** ▓▓▓▓ continuing conduct was likely to cause immediate and serious injury to a client or to the public," said the release provided by J. Anthony McLain of the Alabama Bar.

No information was available on the conduct which caused the suspension and no date was given when ▓▓▓▓ can resume his law practice.

No one answered the telephone at ▓▓▓▓ office, 2813 8th St.

TUSCALOOSA NEWS
FRIDAY APRIL 4, 1997

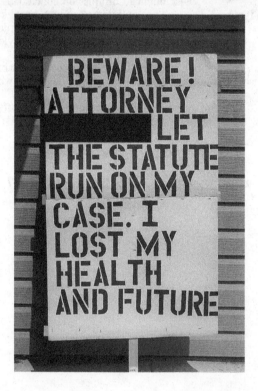

ALABAMA STATE BOARD OF MEDICAL EXAMINERS
EXECUTIVE DIRECTOR

P. O. BOX 946
MONTGOMERY, ALABAMA 36101-0946
848 WASHINGTON AVE.
MONTGOMERY, ALABAMA 36104

TELEPHONE
(334) 242-4116

September 27, 1995

Dear Mr. Hardin:

The Alabama Board of Medical Examiners, at its September 20, 1995, meeting considered your correspondence of July 21, 1995, relative to your allegations that Dr. Bobo was not treating you in a manner that was in the best interest of your health. They also considered a report of the investigation into your request for your complaint to be revisited.

Based upon the information presented the Board could find no new evidence or support to reopen the investigation into the allegations you previously made relative to Dr. Bobo's care and treatment of you.

If you have any questions please contact this office.

Sincerely,
AL BOARD OF MEDICAL EXAMINERS

Chapter 7
Transcending the Bounds of the Ordinary

"Competence" is a term that everyone should take seriously. Tragically, its antitheses – negligence, carelessness, dismissiveness, and *in*competence – prevail all too frequently. My story flows from error, which cannot and must not be excused as a byproduct of the human condition – particularly when lives are at stake. I could wish for nothing more than to write a narrative that extols the virtues of humanity– an account that glorifies its attributes, instead of highlights its iniquities; but I would be remiss were I to sweep my experiences with injustice under the rug, especially when considering those who have fought and sacrificed for our freedoms and have come home, expecting to be treated fairly under the law, only to be disillusioned by apathetic legal and healthcare systems - not once, but over and over again.

As I became more and more subjected to indescribably torturous pain, I began to wonder what my next move should be. No longer was I a superman in training. I felt as though I had the weight of the world on my shoulders, withstanding pain that would make any man scream. I, however, had been exposed to alarming situations, difficult to depict in words – WMD that could make the planet a thing of history. Innately, therefore, I felt that, due to my experiences, I had transcended the bounds of temporal resilience. With each instance of inexplicable pain, combined with my undiagnosed PTSD, I mustered my inner strength, grit my teeth, and defied the ordinary.

Without answers, I felt stymied. As I alluded to earlier, aside from my diagnosis of Grade 1 spondylolisthesis, I also had a congenital birth defect known as spina bifida occulta – an area in my last vertebra that never fused together. From my pre-employment spine x-ray, the L5 failure to fuse was obvious; therefore, the defect did, in fact, contribute to the x-ray's "class C" status). Of course, I didn't become aware of the defect until it was too late.

As I later discovered, individuals with spina bifida occulta will, in most cases, remain asymptomatic (and, hence, problem-free) from childhood into adulthood (as I did). The defect often appears in an x-ray, taken for an unrelated reason. However, in the presence of spina bifida oculta, patients with existing back pain can experience an exacerbation of distress. Therefore, but for the fact that the Plant required me to lift and handle four to six tons every shift (which includes associated equipment) and the concomitant onset of my pain, I would never have endured the onslaught of difficulties that radically changed my entire life-course; and, but for Ron's negligence in allowing the statute of limitations to run on my possible lawsuits, I would not have had any impediments to establishing legal causation between Dr. Bobo's mishandling of my care (i.e., he ignored my orthopedist's advice, even though he was aware of my ongoing trauma and need for treatment during every shift) and the ruination of my future. It was all a random toss of the dice, and outcomes were, tragically, out of my control.

Simple movements and/or activities that involved standing, sitting, bending or twisting – particularly for protracted periods - wreaked physical havoc upon me, and I was at a complete loss as to where to turn. Then, about two years after my surgery, my Dad made a startling discovery. He read a newspaper article which revealed that the pedicle screws placed in my back during spinal fusion surgery had not been approved for Grade 1 spondylolisthesis. However, the FDA had, in fact, approved the screws for patients with Grades 3 and 4, involving vertebral and neurological risk factors far greater than mine. In December, 1995, the Public Citizen advocacy organization warned the FDA against its off-label use of the devices for spondylolisthesis and other spinal conditions, for which there were no apparent benefits, and denounced pedicle screw manufacturers for flagrantly disregarding U.S. and FDA laws.[8] A majority of patients who had the unapproved screws surgically placed in their spines had to go on disability immediately. As for me, my Herculean ability to endure the pain was, in large measure, due to the existence of my undiagnosed PTSD, which fed my physical torture.

Because of such egregious human errors and blatant dismissals of protocol, I experienced physical anguish that defied description. I suspect that, over time, the screws migrated slightly and had begun moving closer to and touching my spinal nerves. This was, possibly, caused by weight-bearing which, in turn, produced pseudoarthrosis (a "false bone" movement of two bones against one another, generated by spinal instability, creating an area that never heals). Such movements may have compounded my difficulties with the pedicle screws used to fuse my spine. Despite the pain, I knew that I had to be mentally proactive. Therefore, while still availing myself of pain management, I made several appointments with specialists, requesting surgical removal of the pedicle screws; but given the fear of permanent neurological damage – and, possibly, paralysis - it was extremely difficult to find a surgeon willing to perform the procedure.

During that time, my mind wandered back to my work at the Plant and, once again, questions swarmed my brain: Why had the Plant's former physician (Dr. Bobo's predecessor) authorized the nurse to sign off on the report, "class B, OK to work?" Why was *his* signature not affixed to that document? Why had I been approved to work when, in fact, I had a "class C" x-ray? Why did my employer fail to provide assistance, other than two days of workers compensation? In the fall of 1994, I attempted to find answers. On

---

8 Laurel S. Mendelson. (1995, December 29). Comments on the FDA's Proposed Classification of Pedicle Screw Spinal Systems (HRG Publication #1383). Public Citizen. Retrieved June 8, 2012, from http://www.citizen.org/publications/publicationredirect.cfm?ID=5543.

September 13, I went to the Plant's former physician's office to ask why he had authorized me to work. "That is not my signature, and I never approved you to work," he assured me. As my suspicion grew, I approached the Montgomery Nurses Board and requested an investigation of the RN's possible forgery; but, again, I was told that too much time had elapsed for such an inquiry. The statute of limitations always seemed to toll – and so did the bell – on my once promising future.

In a last ditch effort to hold expose the Plant's negligence, I appealed to the attorney who had assisted in my claims against Ron. On October 25, 1994, the attorney wrote to Mr. H., the Plant's lawyer, inquiring about my former employer's omission to help me. The following reply was dispatched on November 16, 1994: "Mr. Hardin would have been covered by the company's health insurance policy through the date of his separation from employment. Since that time, he has made no request of this company for any medical treatment." That was an out-and-out lie. As I mentioned, I sought assistance from the Plant's personnel office on two occasions, once on April 17, 1990, well before I left the Plant in 1991. Also, the nurses on duty knew of my injury and severe distress, as I had to spend time in their office with ice on my back after every shift. To say that I never requested help, therefore, was an outrage. So, there I was, entrapped and holding my body's painful weight, with the ardent hope that, somehow, a solution would be forthcoming. Without legal or medical recourse, however, I had to be the artisan of my fate. But *how*?

Because of my undiagnosed PTSD and excruciating pain, I was concerned that I wouldn't be able to pursue and earn a livelihood. At my young age (I was thirty-three at the time), with my entire future spread out before me, that was a devastating prospect. Owing to all of my disciplined military training, I once enjoyed more control over my life than most people can hope to attain. I also had $62,000 in investments, which I had amassed by the time

I was twenty-eight - all of which were quickly depleted by medical bills and living expenses. Without any assistance, at the mercy of pain and undiagnosed PTSD combined, I was too distraught to manage my finances and, eventually, went bankrupt on $70,000, due to an emotional crisis of enormous magnitude.

After close to a year of unemployment, acknowledging my state of isolation (emotional support was non-existent during this time), I literally picked myself up and looked for a job at a local poison control center, manning the phones as an RN. I was excited to work in my field and not have to worry about lifting patients and, possibly, exacerbating my back injury. My genuine interest in the job made for a fulfilling experience, but the physical distress caused by sitting for long periods of time was unstoppable. When I sat for an entire shift, my pain level often escalated to a chronic "8" to "9" on the universal pain scale (which is worse than an acute "10"). Notwithstanding my woeful state, I was able to concentrate and perform the requisites of the job without revealing the extent to which I was suffering. This fact proved that PTSD vets with severe unassociated injuries can push themselves beyond the limits of human strength and endurance; but, as it did for me, that ability comes at an enormous cost.

Although my sharp, shooting back pains had subsided since the surgery, the feeling of nerve damage was becoming more acute. I often heard and read about people who couldn't live with the kind of agony that I endured. "Pedicle screws: the most horrendous invention known to man, definitely a taste of what hell will be like," one patient wrote – a profoundly moving testimony of what I could only feel. All words failed me, as I went into 24/7 survival mode (which I still experience, to this day) – a relentless feeling of internal numbness, defensiveness, and shock.

The potential adverse effects of pedicle screw use cannot be overstated. Below is a list of just some of the possible neurological risks and pitfalls to the insertion of the screws.[9] It is important to note that the following information, taken directly from the Medtronic website, is neither intended as medical advice nor indication of how a given patient will react to the use and insertion of the screws. Every patient is unique and treatment must be carefully undertaken by a physician who will determine the appropriateness of surgery based on the totality of the circumstances in each case.

Contraindications

The contraindications of pedicle screws include, but are not limited to:

- Active infectious process or significant risk of infection (immunocompromise).
- Signs of local inflammation.
- Fever or leukocytosis.
- Morbid obesity.
- Pregnancy.
- Mental illness.

Grossly distorted anatomy caused by *congenital abnormalities* (emphasis added).

- Any other medical or surgical condition which would preclude the potential benefit of spinal implant surgery, such as the presence of congenital abnormalities, elevation of sedimentation rate unexplained by other diseases, elevation of white blood count (WBC), or a marked left shift in the WBC differential count.
- Suspected or documented metal allergy or intolerance.
- Any case not needing a bone graft and fusion.
- Any case where the implant components selected for use

---

9 Medtronic For Healthcare Professionals (2012). Indications, Safety, and Warnings. Retrieved June 15, 2012, from http://www.medtronic.com/for-healthcare-professionals/products-therapies/spinal-orthopedics/posterior-occipitocervical-upper-thoracic-reconstruction-systems/vertex-select-reconstruction-system/indications-safety-and-warnings/index.htm.

would be too large or too small to achieve a successful result.

- Any patient having inadequate tissue coverage over the operative site or inadequate bone stock or quality.
- Any patient in which implant utilization would interfere with anatomical structures or expected physiological performance.
- Any patient unwilling to follow postoperative instructions.
- Any case not described in the indications.

  N.B.: Although not absolute contraindications, conditions to be considered as potential factors for not using this device include:

- Severe bone resorption.
- Osteomalacia.
- Severe osteoporosis.

Potential Adverse Events

- All of the possible adverse events associated with spinal fusion surgery without instrumentation are possible. With instrumentation, a listing of potential adverse events includes, but is not limited to:
- Early or late loosening of any or all of the components.
- Disassembly, bending, and/or breakage of any or all of the components.
- Foreign body (allergic) reaction to implants, debris, corrosion products (from crevice, fretting, and/or general corrosion), including metallosis, staining, tumor formation, and/or autoimmune disease.
- Pressure on the skin from component parts in patients with inadequate tissue coverage over the implant possibly causing skin penetration, irritation, fibrosis, necrosis, and/or

pain. Bursitis. Tissue or nerve damage caused by improper positioning and placement of implants or instruments.

- Post-operative change in spinal curvature, loss of correction, height, and/or reduction.
- Infection.
- Dural tears, pseudomeningocele, fistula, persistent CSF leakage, meningitis.
- Loss of neurological function (e.g., sensory and/or motor), including paralysis (complete or incomplete), dysesthesias, hyperesthesia, anesthesia, paresthesia, appearance of radiculopathy, and/or the development or continuation of pain, numbness, neuroma, spasms, sensory loss, tingling sensation, and/or visual deficits.
- Neuropathy, neurological deficits (transient or permanent), paraplegia, paraparesis, reflex deficits, irritation, arachnoiditis, and/or muscle loss.
- Urinary retention or loss of bladder control or other types of urological system compromise.
- Scar formation possibly causing neurological compromise or compression around nerves and/or pain.
- Fracture, microfracture, resorption, damage, or penetration of any spinal bone (including the sacrum, pedicles, and/or vertebral body) and/or bone graft or bone graft harvest site at, above, and/or below the level of surgery. Retropulsed graft.
- Herniated nucleus pulposus, disc disruption or degeneration at, above, or below the level of surgery.
- Non-union (or pseudarthrosis). Delayed union. Malunion.
- Loss of or increase in spinal mobility or function.
- Inability to perform the activities of daily living.
- Bone loss or decrease in bone density, possibly caused by stresses shielding.

- Graft donor site complications including pain, fracture, or wound healing problems.
- Ileus, gastritis, bowel obstruction or loss of bowel control or other types of gastrointestinal system compromise.
- Hemorrhage, hematoma, occlusion, seroma, edema, hypertension, embolism, stroke, excessive bleeding, phlebitis, wound necrosis, wound dehiscence, damage to blood vessels, or other types of cardiovascular system compromise.
- Reproductive system compromise, including sterility, loss of consortium, and sexual dysfunction.
- Development of respiratory problems, e.g., pulmonary embolism, atelectasis, bronchitis, pneumonia, etc.
- Change in mental status.
- Death.

Note: Additional surgery may be necessary to correct some of these potential adverse events.

There must also be a warning label, placed conspicuously on the box, which specifically mentions the use of pedicle screws only in cases of severe spondylolithesis (Grades 3 and 4) of the L5-S1 vertebra and degenerative spondylolisthesis, with objective evidence of other neurological impairments.[10] As I mentioned, I had Grade 1 spondylolisthesis, with a couple of the milder complications listed above. Given the presence of my congenital defect, the insertion of the screws was contraindicated and , therefore caused many of these complications and my ability to twist, stoop, stand/ or sit for longer periods never improved but worsened.

Fortunately, after about another year of searching for help, I found a surgeon who agreed to remove the pedicle screws. Tests were performed, and I was given the go-ahead. My boss complained that I had not provided my two-week leave request. I

---

10 Id.

explained that my emergency surgery prevented me from giving notice. That's how extreme my situation was.

Prior to surgery, I did something inconceivable for one in my physical condition. I went out into the woods to learn survival skills, desperately trying to save myself. What I didn't realize was that my private battle had just begun, triggering a fight-or-flight response that exceeded the tolerance of ordinary mortals.

PEDICLE SCREW MANUFACTURERS HAVE SHOWN BLATANT DISREGARD OF U.S. LAW AND FDA REGULATIONS BY OPENLY AND ILLEGALLY PROMOTING OFF-LABEL USE OF THESE DEVICES

Senior officials at the FDA have known about the illegal promotion and overuse of pedicle screw systems since 1985, yet no civil or criminal actions have been brought against any manufacturer. According to Dr. Larson (1994), who was intimately involved in the regulation of pedicle screw products by the FDA,

"...[manufacturers] and the medical device industry have actively promoted pedicle screw devices in derogation of the Medical Device Amendments to the Food, Drug, and Cosmetic Act, and in reckless disregard for the fact that they have never been able to demonstrate with scientifically valid data or evidence that these devices were safe of effective for spinal fusion surgery.

"....All of the FDA's clearance and classification decisions are based upon the intended use of the device as represented to us by the manufacturer or device proponent. If the device is promoted for a use other than that which is represented to be its intended use and which serves as a basis for Pre-Market approval or 510(k) clearance, then that device is considered misbranded or adulterated in violation of federal law.

"The FDA's position on pedicle screw devices has consistently been that these devices are significant risk Class III investigational devices which require an IDE and Pre-Market Approval. There has never been sufficient safety and efficacy data provided to allow such approval.

"As of the present date, no pedicle screw manufacturer has been able to successfully complete a clinical trial under an IDE which has led to Pre-Market Approval of any pedicle screw device. Accordingly, there are no legally marketed pedicle screw devices in this county at present, nor has there ever been any demonstrated to be reasonably safe and effective for pedicle fixation" (Larson, 1994).

The FDA's position regarding these devices was further established in a letter to the American Academy of Orthopedic Surgeons dated July 13,1993. That letter stated:

"....In this case the Medical Device Amendments are clear in language and intent. New intended uses and new [pedicle screw systems] pose a potentially significant risk to patients and are automatically classified as class III devices and may only be marketed (and promoted for new uses) after agency approval of a Pre-Market application (PMA). Since 1984 the FDA has repeatedly informed sponsors of such products of the classification status and the conditions under which these new devices could be clinically investigated to determine their safety and effectiveness. Beginning in 1988, FDA has further notified sponsors of screw and plate medical device products submitted through the 510(k) process of the classification of vertebral pedicle screws, limitations imposed on labelling, promotion and marketing for devices such as bone screws, inter-vertebral body screws, sacral screws, iliac screws, bone plates, and spinal fixation systems incorporating bone screws. These 510(k) letters now also include notice of what would constitute adulteration or misbranding of approved devices. In sum, there are no legally marketed bone plates, bone screws, spinal screws, pedicle screws, or device systems that incorporate bone screws commercially available in the United States, that have been cleared or approved for spinal fixation when used for attachment through the pedicle of a vertebra" (Larson, 1994).

3,000 lawsuits against implant manufacturers have already been consolidated in multidistrict litigation claiming injured patients were not informed of the risks, off-label use, or investigational status of pedicle screw systems (Levin, 1995). In the two most recent quarters for which we have data (April-September, 1995), 64 Medical Device Reports about pedicle screws were submitted to the FDA. As is the case with most medical devices, this number probably represents less than 10% of the problems actually encountered.

We have recently obtained new information that reinforces our concerns about pedicle screw spinal systems. Further review of published literature and affidavit testimony from the pending multidistrict litigation In Re: Orthopedic "Bone Screw" Products Liability Litigation, MDL Docket No. 1014, have provided us with material that substantiates our concerns and raises additional questions about the actual rate of complications associated with pedicle screws.

We therefore reiterate our previous recommendations and urge the FDA to retain the Class III status of pedicle screw systems—thereby restricting their sale and use until they have been proven to be safe and effective for the indications for which they are widely used.

PEDICLE SCREWS HAVE NEVER BEEN PROVEN TO ENHANCE SPINAL FUSION OR IMPROVE CLINICAL OUTCOMES OF FUSION SURGERY

The Historical Cohort Study

The Historical Cohort Study formed the basis both for the Orthopedic and Rehabilitation Devices Panel's recommendation to down-classify pedicle screws for the treatment of degenerative spondylolisthesis and spinal fracture and for the FDA's proposal to expand the use of the devices for the treatment of acute and chronic instabilities and deformities (Federal Register, 10/4/95). But this study should support no such conclusions because it contains systemic errors in methodology and interpretation. These errors are so significant that the cohort study seems to have been designed in order to support the down-classification of pedicle screws from class III to class II--rather than to evaluate the outcomes of pedicle screw systems. With its biased approach, faulty methods and interpretations, and lack of peer review, the study appears to be more a large-scale advertisement for pedicle screws than a valid piece of scientific evidence.

Issues in Study Design

From the outset, the historical cohort study was described as an opportunity to vindicate pedicle screw spinal systems. According to the authors, the purpose of the cohort study was to provide the FDA with valid scientific evidence "to determine that pedicle screws could be considered as class II devices, rather than class III devices" (Yuan, Garfin, Dickman, & Mardjetko, 1994). This lack of objectivity is unacceptable; no scientific study should be designed to prove a predetermined outcome.

Issues in Study Methods

The methods used in this study were inadequate to collect the information needed to draw conclusions about the safety and effectiveness of pedicle screw systems. Several of the problems with the study's methodology are discussed below.

First, the patient-inclusion criteria were poorly defined. Only patients with diagnoses of degenerative spondylolisthesis or spinal fracture were included in this study. But degenerative spondylolisthesis is a poorly-defined term that can mean any type of displacement of the lumbar vertebrae caused by the

Chapter 8
Living In Two Worlds

Once I acknowledged that a second surgery to remove the pedicle screws from my back was inevitable, all I could think was, "Not again! How could this be happening?" Sometimes, I felt as though God had abandoned me, and that I was walking alone through an endless maze of torment and tribulation. Deep inside, however, I knew that God was always there, guiding my path; and, with each step I took, I became a better Christian - even if I couldn't feel or sense His presence. As the poem "Footprints In the Sand" suggests, God must have been carrying me, because I was so ill, that I lost my contact with Him. That's how I felt, anyway. Before all of my trials began, my faith had been somewhat tenuous. As time passed, however, though I didn't regularly attend structured religious services, I prayed (as I still do today) in the quietude of my home, in my own way and in my own words, asking for healing, peace of mind, and a life that I had envisioned before my world came crashing down – a life filled with activity and socialization.

One facet of my personality which even the most trying of circumstances never could quell was my motivation to utilize my acquired knowledge and skills in the service of others. Given the fact that I had so much trouble sitting (even when my employer gave me a special chair to accommodate my back pain), I applied for jobs where I wouldn't have to sit for most of the day. In furtherance of that objective, I sent applications to a list of hospitals, including the Veterans Administration; and, each time an employer turned me down, I made note of the rejections. To fortify myself against discrimination, I researched the provisions of the Americans With Disabilities Act ("the ADA") and the Equal Opportunity Employment Commission ("the EEOC"). However, as I soon learned, rejection can be masked as reasonable justification, depending upon the how the interviewer couches his or her questions. One would think that, as a VA patient, I would have been given a preference; but I was turned down, after all. I never revealed my physical limitations because I knew that, if I did, I wouldn't be hired. In all events, according to the ADA, I was not required to disclose my physical challenges, and prospective employers could not broach the subject.

A similar scenario took place when I applied for employment with an automobile company. There, my evaluation consisted of manual dexterity tests, a written examination and a phone interview, the latter of which took place toward the end of the hiring process. Once I reached that stage, the woman to whom I spoke asked me specific questions. Although I realized that honest answers would not produce a callback, I simply couldn't lie. If I had, and someone just happened to discover my deliberate evasion of the truth, I would have been denied the job. To be sure, I didn't want that to happen. So, I braced myself, and prepared to answer in straightforward fashion.

"Can you explain why there is a year's gap in your employment history?" The interviewer asked.

"I had back surgery during that year," I replied.

"Were you out for the whole year?"

"The better part of it."

Because I was a medical professional, and due to my experiences at the Plant, I knew very well that my answers would raise a red flag for the type of job that I was seeking. I also was aware that, most likely, the modern factory had many jobs available that I could handle with reasonable accommodations. At a later point in time, I visited the factory and discovered that, in fact, my hunch was valid. My primary objective was, of course, to find employment that would afford me the opportunity to sit for shorter periods, given my back difficulties. I was not, simply, applying haphazardly for another factory job. Rather, at that point, I was fully aware of my physical challenges and I wanted to be productive, while reasonably accommodating my limitations. Subsequent to the phone interview, I allowed time for a callback which, of course, never came. I then called the EEOC, whose staff investigated my claim, found it to be viable, and issued me a "right to sue" letter from the federal government.

Thereafter, with the correspondence in hand, I went to my new attorney's office in Tuscaloosa, and commenced an action against the Plant. The case went to federal court and, upon reviewing all of the evidence, the federal judge threw out my claim, stating that I was not disabled! At that point, I was at my wit's end, speechless and feeling that I was out on a limb without a safety net. How could such a result ensue? To say that I was not disabled with the unapproved pedicle screws in my back was utterly ludicrous! This was a quintessential example of evasion and corruption. Where was justice? I asked myself, searching in vain for plausible answers. My attorney was not willing to appeal, believing that it wasn't worth pursuing; but how was that possible, when I had endured major back surgery, and was living every day with unspeakable distress, compounded by undiagnosed PTSD?

Meanwhile, for what seemed like an eternity, I was hanging on by a fingernail at work. My job entailed receiving phone calls from beleaguered parents whose children ingested toxic substances, answering their questions, and providing assistance. For about five years, while at the poison control center, I was documented as the fastest worker on staff. Without even looking at the records, I knew that I was ahead of all the other nurses – and I was determined to remain so. That was, simply, my modus operandi, which mirrored my mission to stay one step ahead of my Soviet counterpart at all times. In both cases, I had to minimize destruction – the possible peril of a child and the potential annihilation of the world. In my mind, both of these dire scenarios converged. Due to my PTSD, I was unable to separate my cognitive regression to the Cold War and the job at hand; and my physical pain only served to compound my agony. Every time the phone rang, I became frantic and tried to hide my reaction from the other nurses; and whenever I heard a child crying in the background, the feeling would turn into panic. Many times, I thought that I would have a heart attack and die, right then and there.

Through all of my anguish, I simply went through the motions, internally fighting with myself, while my body – once my greatest ally – was constantly betraying me. At one point, while I was sitting at my desk, I had an extreme PTSD episode, which necessitated a visit to the emergency room. I thought that I was having a cardiac arrest; but, fortunately, I recovered and was able to return to work. My extremely heightened stress level also caused innumerable intestinal issues (specifically, irritable bowel syndrome or "IBS"). Because my condition was so severe, nothing (not even medication) could prevent the onslaught of discomfort that I experienced on a daily basis. I just had to deal with my symptoms in the best way possible, under the circumstances. I must say that I put on a very good front – without knowledge that I was, in fact, doing anything of the sort. Once a superman in training, I was now teaching the Master Class. Many people in my position have been known to commit suicide, unable to cope with the enormous stress and concomitant fight-or-flight symptoms - the moment-by-moment struggle to survive.

Always hoping to find solutions, I went in for surgery to remove the pedicle screws. Nearly five years had passed since my first operation in 1992, and although I was aware of the risks involved, I was willing to take the chance of feeling slightly to moderately improved. As it turned out, the second surgery was not quite as traumatic as the first, and had a shorter recovery time – about four to six weeks. From a CAT scan and my doctor's own assessment, however, the pedicle screws were touching the nerves in my spine and may have been rubbing against them. At that time, I didn't know the long-term effects and what the extent of the damage would be.

As the pain relentlessly continued, I resolved that *someone* had to be held accountable for my suffering. An individual doesn't just go through life in constant pain and torment without an anchor – a means by which to seek redress. Certainly, I could not, justifiably, point fingers at my surgeon. He could not be held responsible for the regulatory status of the pedicle screws any more than for his use of sutures, knee and hip implants, and other materials left in the body during surgery. Doctors are only expected to attend seminars, in order to receive instructions on how to use their equipment. The flagrant gross negligence that ensued in my case – and many others – regarding the off-label use of the pedicle screws derived from the manufacturer of those devices, who failed to heed the FDA's warning.

So, once again, in resorting to the legal system, I brought an action against the manufacturer. My attorney initially sued for three million dollars. At the deposition, when the opposing counsel asked me to describe my pain subsequent to the insertion of the pedicle screws, I began to sob. My reaction was so intense and unexpected, that I, myself, was shocked. The entire episode was an enormous embarrassment for me, a stoic serviceman who rarely displayed feelings of duress; but I was being asked to explain something that literally defied adjectives. Noting my distress, my attorney and the opposing counsel suggested that I take a break and go into the bathroom. I conceded and, when I returned, I had regained my composure; but when the question was presented to me a second time, my emotions resurfaced and I began to cry again.

The most accurate way to describe the pain was to analogize it to having my finger stuck in a wall socket, on and off, 24/7, with my undiagnosed PTSD only making matters worse. I felt as though I were being assaulted and, in the process, I became a man without a country, living in two worlds – the world of conventional mores, where injustice prevailed at every turn, and a world in which I constantly fortified myself, in every possible way, with survival strategies. It is no exaggeration to state that I was perpetually at war, readying myself…for what? I could not begin to explain, and I had no idea whether my day of victory would ever come. Although I was inwardly ready for surrender, I never displayed the white flag – even in the worst of times – and even though I had no idea when or if an allied rescue would come.

OPERATION NOTE

NAME: HARDIN, GREGORY   MED.REC.NO.: 1072011   ROOM:

SURG: MARK N. HADLEY, M.D.   ASSIST: ROBERT D. ROBINSON, M.D.

SURG.SIGN.: _____ M1t _____

DATE OPER.: 09/16/97   ADMITTED: / /   DISCHARGED: / /

SERVICE: MARK N. HADLEY, M.D.   DICTATED: 09/17/97   TRANSCRIBED: 09/17/97

DOCTOR/SERV.SIGN.: _____ M1t _____

PREOPERATIVE DIAGNOSIS: Failure of internal fixation hardware
                          with persistent L5, S1 radiculopathy.

POSTOPERATIVE DIAGNOSIS: Same.

OPERATION: 1. Re-exploration L5, S1.
                          2. Removal of failed internal fixation
                              hardware.
                          3. Left-sided lateral recess
                              decompression at L4-5 and L5, S1 with
                              decompression of exiting L5 and S1
                              nerve roots.

ANESTHESIA: General with endotracheal intubation.

INDICATIONS: This is a 35-year-old male who had spinal
instability. He had this treated with a 5-1 stabilization
infusion construct. Unfortunately he has developed horrible and
horrific back pain and left leg symptoms and signs. Workup
reveals that his internal fixation construct appears to be
misplaced. It also appears to be much too long compromising the
4-5 facet complex, particularly on the left. He appears to have
significant lateral recess compromise of both the L5 and S1 nerve
roots left which is where he is mostly symptomatic. The patient
is a candidate for removal of his internal fixation hardware. He
does not appear to have spinal instability at this point. He is a
candidate for decompression of the L5, S1 nerve roots on the left
in hopes that we can provide him benefit. He understands the
risks of the procedure as well as technique. He wished to
proceed. Consent is obtained.

PROCEDURE: After smooth induction of anesthesia and intubation,
the patient was moved from the hospital bed to the operating table
and placed in a prone position on a Wilson frame. The patient's
lumbosacral spine region was shaved, prepped and draped in the
usual sterile fashion. The previous skin incision was opened.

Chapter 9
A Suit of Armor

*I*t's hard to live in two worlds, yet on the edge of nowhere, in disbelief, and without recourse. After the surgery, I felt that I had taken as much abuse as I possibly could stand, and my undiagnosed PTSD was exacerbating my every feeling of distress. I simply could not get my head around the fact that I had sacrificed so much for my country and that I was being denied the very liberties that I had steadfastly strived to preserve. Although I earnestly sought help, no one was paying any attention.

In my already confused and tortured state, the ultimate injustice surfaced when I learned that the federal judge presiding over my case against the pedicle screw manufacturer dismissed the suit. His reasoning: the screws were neither bent nor broken. What incomprehensible disrespect and irresponsibility – yet again – on the part of the legal system! The issue was not the condition of the screws at all, but the fact that their off-label use had not been FDA approved and would, most likely, cause more problems, including nerve damage. Already baffled and negated unfairly, I was primed for bad news. To say that I was a "wounded warrior" only begins to touch upon my indescribable state.

The Wounded Warrior Project expounds the notion that "the greatest casualty is being forgotten." Indeed, injured vets are often a forgotten population. Society's dismissal of these individuals is the most egregious wrongdoing. I was – and am – a part of that subculture of forgotten men and women, endlessly struggling to put one foot in front of the other – or, for that matter, to sit and contemplate my anguish. Still, I ardently believe that my voice must be heard and, after all is said and done, free expression is worth the price of my physical pain - which I experience even now, as I write.

After the pedicle screws were removed, I endured a significant level of chronic pain, which, to this day, has endured. At work, I was sitting for ten hours a day, which included my two-hour work commute. Persistent nerve damage pain ran down my legs, while my PTSD, yet undiagnosed and untreated, made me jumpy and hypervigilant (which, to the untrained eye, spelled "paranoia"). I perspired all the time and suffered from anxiety, which manifested in feelings of vulnerability and agoraphobia (fear of leaving the house). At that point, because I had been repeatedly abused and tortured by inept, corrupt legal and medical system(s), I was like a scared, wounded animal, almost retreating from help, unable to trust anyone. Each time I tried to get assistance, my efforts were in vain and my voice went unheeded. Therefore, because of the PTSD and trauma, I pulled away. All the while, my survival mode was at work, manifesting in constant alertness to danger.

In the presence of people who had no conception of hardship, I tried to act casual and "normal" (however the term is defined by those who do not live with my kind of challenges). In other situations, I did my best to act as most people would under my circumstances – those who had gone through my level of trauma; but, invariably, I was always alert to even more danger – a call to action.

Desperately wanting to be proactive, I reached out again – this time to the VA research division, in the form of an emotional plea. My letter (sent on April 15, 2000), referring to myself in the third person, appears in pertinent part, below.

THIS IS WHAT MAKES VETERANS HOMELESS

This young man was hired by BF Goodrich ("the Plant"), which knew about his congenital birth defect, as it was revealed in a pre-employment x-ray and a radiologist's report in the company's possession. After a while, he was placed on a heavy labor job, physically handling 4-6 tons per 8-hour shift, which he would not have started, had he known about his birth defect. While working full-time, he was attending college, using his GI Bill funds, and had a promising future. Not long into this job, he injured his back, due to the heavy labor, coupled with the congenital spine defect (spondylolisthesis and spina bifida occulta). Ultimately, as a result of his injury, he lost his job.

Prior to his employment at the Plant, this young man served his country as a Nuclear Missile Systems Analyst, and literally helped to keep America out of a nuclear exchange with Russia during the Cold War (from 1980-1984), when the Doomsday Clock was three and four minutes to midnight. Because he did not become aware of the birth defect until after his injury and needed help with his ensuing medical expenses, he retained the services of an attorney.

After numerous consultations and plans to institute an action against the Plant and, possibly, the doctor who allowed the injury to worsen, he learned that the attorney had allowed the statute of limitations to toll on both potential law suits. He then reported the attorney to the state bar, and was notified that the attorney had, in fact, mishandled his case. Thirty different attorneys, including counsel assigned to pursue a legal malpractice claim, let the statute run because the attorney did not have malpractice insurance.

The young man also reported the Plant's physician to the Medical Examiners Board for failing to limit him to light duty, as his orthopedic doctor had advised in writing. The medical records substantiating these claims were mysteriously burned in a fire.

After the medical and legal malpractice cases were prevented by the statute's tolling, the young man began picketing the attorney's and Plant physician's office, warning the public. He did not want history to repeat itself for anyone else. The attorney and the doctor didn't have any legal recourse against the young man, because he did not engage in defamation. He only spoke the truth. The man sent a picture of himself picketing at the doctor's office to the Medical Examiners Board, but he received no reply.

At about this time, the state bar suspended the license of the above-mentioned attorney because he had a history of malfeasance and was labeled "a danger to society" in the Tuscaloosa News. This was little consolation to the young man, whose nightmare had just begun.

His injury at the Plant warranted surgery. Soon thereafter, he learned that the pedicle screws inserted in his spine were experimental and were never approved by the FDA. The screws made a bad condition much worse, and caused significant neurological damage. Soon after this discovery, the man consulted with another attorney to pursue a suit for compensatory damages against the pedicle screw's manufacturer for promoting their off-label use against FDA approval. It took years for the man to find a doctor to take them out, because doctors feared that his condition would worsen.

Four and a half years after filing the suit, the young man learned that the federal judge presiding over the case threw it out because the screws were not bent or damaged. That was not the reason for the lawsuit. Rather, the issue was the manufacturer's promotion of the screws' off-label use, contrary to FDA approval. His significant nerve damage contributed to wrecking his life.

At that point, the man had endured torture and trauma that ruined every aspect of his life. Through no fault of his own, he lost his health, career, future family life, $30,000 in retirement and $32,000 in savings. Before his first surgery, he did receive his RN degree, but is very limited as to what he can do in the field. He would have felt better about the whole thing if he had suffered an accident or had been able to get some help.

The legal system has failed this veteran over and over again, and left him with a life of struggle. Can we stand by and watch our veterans pay the price for liberty and justice for all and offer them none? The land has become lawless, and there is no accountability. This young man is now looking to the America he defended from nuclear attack for help because it is difficult to help himself. He feels that he has lost his future and any future family of his own, due to his chronic pain, major depression, emotional problems, and borderline-bankrupt status. It is the responsibility of all Americans to make sure that our veterans are treated fairly under the law. Does anyone care? He desperately needs a break.

Thank you,
Greg Hardin

I was "this young man" - too physically and emotionally anguished to own my truth in writing. This young man was wearing a suit of armor, impervious to the magnitude of his own suffering, for he was superman; and this young man finally was about to face his diagnosis of Post Traumatic Stress Disorder. After reviewing the letter, the first question that the VA research doctor asked was, "What does your house look like?" I replied that it was a wreck. That revelation, coupled with my omniscient third person account, led her to a finding of PTSD. When the doctor had, at last, labeled my condition, I didn't feel any sense of alarm – perhaps because, as things stood up until that point, I was in a perpetual state of hyperawareness and vigilance – as I still am today, now with greater awareness of my condition and its cause.

After that conversation, not much more was said about the diagnosis, since people in my circle of family and friends didn't know very much about it. In fact, some people made the mistake of thinking that I was just "crazy;" but that wasn't the case at all. Most people fear what they do not understand and, out of misapprehension, tend to form erroneous misconceptions. In my case, people's reaction was nondescript, probably because they thought I might snap.

From my personal perspective, however, the issue of my state of mind was superseded by my desire to blend into the so-called "everyday" paradigm in which everyone else lived; but, as mentioned, I was living in two worlds, unable to fully integrate into society, due to my conditioning. I was, simply, different, no matter how hard I tried to assimilate. In that struggle, my VA PTSD doctor provided an interesting take on the matter. He told me that I was the one who lived in "the real world," while others did not; and that is why my behavior seemed strange to those who didn't have knowledge of what I was going through. In other words, my reaction to external stimuli was more acute and sensitized than most people without PTSD. Although I was extremely agitated, I never had a violent streak. On the contrary, I believed in maintaining respect and trust, at all times, and I will always live by that ideal. Sadly, by ignoring the extent of my struggle, the healthcare and legal systems failed to accord me my due. Through the entire ordeal, my level of trust quickly dwindled.

Trust always was – and remains – a huge component in my life, due to my extreme trauma and the discipline for which I was trained - and with which I continue to live. I realized, therefore, that most people would not react to or treat me in the same manner in which I approached them. This caused me to be very vigilant and wary, and to tread cautiously in all of my dealings. Nonetheless, I, myself, am extremely trustworthy and operate by the Golden Rule at all times, always considering "the other" as myself – only wearing a slightly different suit of armor.

The baseless misinterpretations that surround PTSD (such as the erroneous belief that PTSD vets cannot perform their duties due to stress or serve with distinction – as I and countless others have and continue to do) may ensue from PTSD sufferers' inability to communicate effectively. For example, when I attempted to call my plight to the attention of local and national news, I was extremely hyper, and my speech was fractured, to the point where I had difficulty stringing sentences together. Perhaps because I was falsely perceived as "crazy" or unreliable, I was always relegated to the sidelines and told that my story was "horrible" and "sad," but the media never followed through with an exposé. I suspect that, given Dr. Bobo's influence in my hometown of Tuscaloosa and, since I didn't enjoy celebrity status, I was unable to receive the attention that I – and all of America's veterans – deserve. I was just another soldier, having to deal with my own internal war of nerves, facing personal challenges alone, without help or a true display of gratitude on the part of the government or healthcare and legal structures, purportedly on the side of the public welfare. Why do our veterans fall through the cracks? *All* American servicemen and servicewomen, regardless of such immutable characteristics as race, physical disability, creed or belief system, must be redressed for our sacrifices, which have lifetime repercussions. In the aftermath of our struggle, nothing that we strive for or endeavor to do will ever be without personal, emotional, and financial cost. The least that we can expect from our nation and our government is not just a perfunctory "thank you," but genuine support to assist in moving forward with our lives.

Because the PTSD severely compromised my ability to function productively (a fact which had been corroborated by various medical tests), the VA doctor finally weaned me off of work in 2003. The feeling was incredible, but it was a double-edged sword. On the one hand, I no longer had to put pressure on my back by sitting for what seemed like interminable hours; however, given my loss of earning capacity, I had to make serious adjustments in my life. To say the least, I was frustrated that all of my potential had, essentially, gone by the wayside – my motivation to work, my drive to meaningfully serve humanity, my ability to climb the proverbial ladder of success, to have a wife and family of my own. As things stood, however, I was an island, in the midst of an internal war of emotions, battling anxiety, major depression, physical disability, and debilitation barraging me at every turn – feelings that no one but those who are or have been in my shoes could even begin to understand.

There I stood – and still remain - in my suit of armor, vulnerable and at the mercy of my body and racing mind, imprisoned by the thousand-mile stare, occasioned by the extreme stress that I endured, which led me to block out my surroundings and desensitize myself to my inner torment. At the same time, I was keenly in tune and hypervigilant when dealing with outside stimuli. With each foot in a different zone of existence, I learned to do one little thing at a time - to live life in segments, breaking everything down in my mind, so as not to activate "the big picture" - and, thus, trigger my extreme, unmanageable anxiety. My next step was to seek PTSD treatment at the Veterans Administration; but, as I will recount, it was too little, too late.

Chapter 10
Presentiments of Danger

*H*ardship comes with lessons, and as traumatic as they have been, my own experiences have increased my sense of awareness about myself and my personal requisites for subsisting in daily life. Once I put a label to my hypervigilance, startle responses, and a host of other reactions to external stimuli, I was able to seek treatment. Seeking help does not, necessarily, "cure" one's internal battle of nerves – particularly when the condition is chronic and, like mine, has been ongoing for decades. However, knowledge empowers; and, if my own suffering serves any purpose, it is to reach out and share my experiences with others.

Every day, I live with presentiments of danger – the foreshadowing of what could, potentially, occur to place me in fear of imminent bodily harm or trigger a "fight or flight" response. Even though the event(s) which would precipitate that reaction may never happen, the apprehension is *very real*. The anticipation of that stimulus or occurrence is the source of extreme stress and nervousness. PTSD is an anxiety disorder. Those of us who suffer from the condition might try to smile on the surface, while on a more visceral level, we are under enormous pressure.

Over two decades had passed since the events that caused my PTSD. Therefore, the positive effects of my in-patient program were limited and finite. For about six weeks, I was at the VA hospital, assigned to a room which I shared with a roommate undergoing the same treatment. Two or three doctors evaluated me, and I had to take several exams via a computer. Among other things, the tests evaluated my intellect, memory, and general psychiatric status. The schedule was militaristic. I had to rise early, attend to my assigned chores, and go to breakfast. All of my fellow participants were either from Vietnam or the first Iraq war, and being a noncombatant made me feel like somewhat of an oddity. However, the end goal was the same: to educate us about PTSD.

Some of the courses assisted vets in dealing with substance abuse. When I was in the Air Force, some of the airmen in my job classification smoked pot as a way of dealing with their tremendous stress. I never understood how such capable individuals, entrusted with so much responsibility, could just throw it all away. Through every challenge I had to face, I never resorted to drug use; and, hence, I did not have to attend those classes.

Due to my training in healthcare, I was somewhat more aware than others about what to expect. Consequently, I did not derive as many benefits from the program as those without preexisting knowledge. Although I have defined "post-traumatic stress" throughout this narrative, it is worth summarizing here. PTSD ensues from exposure to a traumatic event, which involves an imminent threat of danger to oneself or others, of a magnitude that surpasses everyday experiences which trigger fear responses. Subsequent to that life-altering event, recurring recollections or "flashbacks" of the event persist. At times, these recurring thoughts or images cause the PTSD sufferer to relive the event, as though it were happening in present time. Typically, when this occurs, the individual seeks avoidance of all stimuli that may cause him or her to react. These include alienation or disassociation from others (i.e., a "numbing" effect), consequent inability to relate to others, a sense of hopelessness, difficulty sleeping, focusing on daily activities, hypervigilance, exaggerated startle responses, hopelessness, paranoia, and concomitant distress, which hampers one's ability to function normally.

As for me, after being physically assaulted by the healthcare system, left out in the cold due to legal negligence, and at the mercy of PTSD on top of everything else, I fell prey to desperation and anxiety. I also suffer with confusion, which is a symptom of PTSD and is experienced by other vets, as well; however, it is unassociated with avoidance of stimuli. What man could take such abuse under the circumstances that I have endured, and not think about defending himself? The problem was that I did not know *how*.

For me, the world is still a dangerous place, and I recognize that the chance of a nuclear nightmare is far greater than most people know. I always said that if Russia and the United States began to throw nuclear weapons around, I would want to be a casualty of one landing right in my front yard, rather than live through the ensuing mayhem. Tragically, my training as a Nuclear Missile Systems Analyst gave me insight into the carnage that potentially could result– and I have lived with that thought for decades. Even now, as I write these lines, I am sweating and my leg is jumping repeatedly.

In my daily life, I try to avoid large gatherings – particularly crowds that might pay any kind of attention to me. My feelings of anxiety manifest in repetitive movements of limbs, and I bite my fingernails. Something as commonplace as climbing a flight of stairs can be a physical trigger for an emotional reaction related to the PTSD. Intense sunlight can cause the same reaction. My startle response is so severe, that it doesn't take much to set off a post-traumatic stress response (such as abrupt, loud, or unexpected noises). Note that the operative word here is "unexpected." If I am at a shooting range, where I anticipate rifle reports, I will not jump because I am braced and ready for the sounds. However, I probably will experience a steady elevation of my stress level when shooting (due, perhaps, to the high level of stimulation). Other triggers for my PTSD are helicopters, jet engines, and certain phone ringers. Movie scenes which depict wartime conflicts or prisoners being tortured can trigger my stress reactions and actually make me sick.

Then, of course, there is emotional numbing – feelings of avoidance and alienation, which consistently sabotage potential or existing relationships. As I have mentioned, my "fight or flight" responses are accompanied by the need to retreat in social situations. My desire to socialize, meet women and, ultimately, have a family are hampered by my war of nerves and its side effects. I have come to realize, however, that when I explain my potential startle reactions, people tend to be less judgmental. Communication is a vital tool for surviving in the world, and I strive every day to enhance that skill.

Another essential ingredient in facing and dealing with PTSD is the act of removing stigmas and taking the condition from obscurity into the public eye. Thankfully, humanitarians like James Gandolfini, award-winning actor of *The Sopranos* fame, are striving to enlighten veterans and civilians, alike about the ravages of PTSD. In 2010, Gandolfini's film, *Wartorn: 1861-2010* aired on HBO, chronicling the lasting devastation wreaked upon veterans and their families throughout American history.[11] The film is a poignant wakeup call to anyone who has ever confronted and formed erroneous judgments about PTSD sufferers and their symptoms. For example, one must not assume that everyone with PTSD is insane or predisposed to violence, unless an individual has clearly displayed a propensity for such behavior or a history of violent tendencies.

Stigmas involving PTSD often derive from the fact that its causes are "invisible." That is, there is no ostensible, tangible evidence of damage directly caused by the condition. Today, however, medical science is eliminating the mystique of PTSD through powerful scans that reveal "hidden" changes in the brain caused by service-related PTSD and traumatic brain injury (TBI).[12] Identify-

---

11 Excerpts of the film and an option to purchase the DVD can be found at: http://www.hbo.com/documentaries/wartorn-1861-2010/index.html#/documentaries/wartorn-1861-2010/index.html

12 Brain Scans reveal Invisible Damage of PTSD. Huffpost Healthy Living. Retrieved July 30, 2012. From http://www.huffingtonpost.com/2009/11/13/brain-scans-reveals-invis_n_355476.html.

ing physical indicators of an otherwise "invisible" disorder somehow gives credence to its existence. Society often hankers after visuals - the "I'll believe it when I see it" mindset. As I've learned, however, believing and seeing do not necessarily occur in tandem; but the fact that PTSD can be documented is sweet vindication for those who, like me, have often heard, "It's all in your head!" Actually, it *is* in my head; but, now, medical evidence points to causally related physical symptoms that were once indefinable.

Having excelled in psychiatric studies, I keenly understand the importance of not making rash assumptions or rushing to judgment. Applying that approach to military PTSD sufferers, their families and friends, I must note here that it is important not to expect too much or place any demands on a PTSD veteran. The individual already under stress must avoid added pressures. Therefore, it is important not to push a conversation or topic that will make the person cognitively revisit that memory or event. Instead, friends and family should monitor the conversation and take visual clues from the individual's expression, body movements, etc.

Writing this book with service-related PTSD has occasioned a veritable implosion of feelings and triggers that have caused me emotional distress and the physical symptoms that necessarily follow in my case. Another vet with PTSD alone - *without* my attendant physical pain - would, justifiably, avoid writing such a book at all cost. However, I chose to endure the stress because the story must be told. This was a personal mission - a chance to air my grievances, and declare that the unfair treatment of our veterans by medical and legal service providers is possibly the worst crime in America today. Our sacrifice must not go unnoticed. Education, attention and *care* are of the essence, and until we receive just treatment, the word "freedom" is mere verbiage, without real substance behind it. I am enraged...and that's not all that I have to say....

Chapter 11
An Open Letter To Those Who Care

Now that I have finally found my voice, I can write in the first person. No longer do I write in the voice of an unnamed individual, to whom I once referred as "this young man." This young man is older now and, over time, has acquired a lot more wisdom and purpose. He has turned into someone who has not only encountered and faced the reality of his suffering, but also has a message: Disabled vets must not continue to be a forgotten population. Many of them will suffer for the rest of their lives, without being afforded fair treatment under the law. This injustice recurs over and over again, undermining the very fabric of our nation.

There is a raging need within me not to be an island, not to endure in silence, but I am still entrapped, hoping to find a way out. I freely acknowledge and own my suffering now, and the most I can do is reach out to others who, like me, have been silenced by a war of nerves. We are alienated from loved ones, unable to sustain personal relationships, physically and emotionally isolated from society, angered by the ill-treatment of government and healthcare, and ignored by the legal system (in my case, at the state and federal levels).

I am one of countless individuals who have sacrificed everything; but, in truth, my story belongs to every serviceman and woman who has ever subordinated personal wellbeing for the sake of his or her country. These pages resonate with an internal battle cry against unnecessary physical pain and the ravages of PTSD, meted upon us by the very institutions that we have served. Writing this book has been incredibly difficult – physically and emotionally. PTSD sufferers are, typically, reticent when speaking out and expressing feelings. Unsettling triggers and stimuli are everywhere. In fact, a thought itself can be an unwanted stimulus that can cause a "fight or flight response" or a cognitive regression to the scene of the disturbing event. For me, everything that I experienced during the Cold War is still very real and present in my life.

To compound matters, my back pain is a daily reminder of what I *cannot* do. I can no longer dance, jet ski, or perform daily activities independently (such as house keeping, lawn mowing, and the like). Before the onset of PTSD, I was a social person by nature, eager to make friends, and join in the mainstream of life. Now, quite against my will, I am an isolationist, and all of my aspirations for family and personal achievement have been vanquished. I cannot help but think about what could have been and, even though I try to dwell in the present, the "what if's" inevitably arise and plague me, at times.

Perhaps, such circumstances would have been made bearable by a helping hand; but each time I reached out for assistance, I was ignored. Many people don't understand the gravity of what I have been through – particularly because I was not on the front lines; but I am here to testify that, each day, I am still at war. The call to launch still looms large in my mind. While others go about their daily lives, I'm braced for an impending nuclear holocaust. In a flash, I can relive it all again – in the sudden occurrence of a sound or other stressor. Sometimes, I wish that I could ask the sun to cease shining. Its heat and glare can sometimes cause me to want to flee – but where?

Yes, I am an island, but now I am armed – fortified in the knowledge that, when islands unite, continents are formed. In deference to my fellow vets, I had hoped to provide a forum for their stories in this narrative. To that end, I ceased the writing process for a period of three months, during which I actively sought out contributors to this text – those who might be willing to share their service-related experiences and the devastating aftermath of PTSD. What I discovered was not at all surprising to me – a pervasive reluctance on the part of servicemen and women to voice their impressions and experiences. The reasons are simple yet, at their core, extremely complex. Those who have served are emotionally overwhelmed, and words elude them. You have to catch us on days when we are willing to talk – and that does not occur very frequently. We experience a torment that never dissipates. In a sense, all of us have forgotten what "normal" is, so that when the doctors asks us how we are doing, we don't have a reference point for comparison - not one that we can recall, anyway. Therefore, we are just going through the motions, day by day – in my case, without any legal or medical help. The physical, psychological, and emotional pain is beyond description. How, then, was I able to even begin to tell my story? The answer lies partially in my medical background and the insights that I gleaned as an R.N. – my personal fascination with and commitment to healthcare. In this writing, I was, in effect, my own patient, desperately trying to view myself objectively, in order to tell my truth.

For most of us in the service, however, the code of silence is a way of life. I spoke with one remarkable man who served in Nuclear Command and Control in Operation Desert Storm. "When I broke my neck," he explained, "I was told to 'shut up.' If I complained, I would have been forced to take mind-altering drugs, and paperwork would have been initiated to discharge me. When I was in charge of training, I had to teach standing up. I was in constant pain; but I never knew what it was doing to me. I was intensely mission-oriented and serious about what I was entrusted to do; but I felt isolated, and I was drinking heavily. Although I finally had to take Oxycodone for pain, never once was I told that it could become addictive."

When asked about his primary objectives as a veterans' advocate, the gentleman replied, "Vets need society to pay attention to them. Military transition programs don't help very much. Vets need to be well-networked, not entrapped in the web of bureaucracy, which treats everyone the same. Yes, there may be commonalities, but each individual has unique potential which must be tapped and recognized. Through individual outreach, genuine understanding, and collaboration with professionals, the truth will come to light; and the truth is that veterans need to vent, they need help, and they need a viable means by which to integrate into society and the nation that they served."

My prayer is that those who care will listen and act. Heroes always do.